True God:
Restoring Your Relationship with Our Creator and Savior

Lindsay Fait

River Birch Press

Daphne, Alabama

True God: Restoring Your Relationship with Our Creator and Savior
by Lindsay Fait
Copyright ©2020 Lindsay Fait

All rights reserved. This book is protected under the copyright laws of the United States of America. This book may not be copied or reprinted for commercial gain or profit.

Scriptures marked NASB are taken from the *New American Standard Bible*, Copyright ©1960, 1962, 1963, 1968, 1971, 1973, 1975, 1977 by The Lockman Foundation.

Scripture quotations marked "NKJV" are taken from the New King James Version®. Copyright © 1982 by Thomas Nelson, Inc. Used by permission. All rights reserved.

ISBN 978-1-951561-18-5 (print)
ISBN 978-1-951561-19-2 (ebook)
For Worldwide Distribution
Printed in the U.S.A.

River Birch Press
P.O. Box 868
Daphne, AL 36526

Table of Contents

Alive *1*
The Brokenness of Creation *4*
God to the Full *6*
Greatest Praise *9*
The Cross Too Heavy to Bear *12*
The Separation Divide *15*
When You Paint the Stars *17*
Who Will Turn Back *20*
Open and Free *23*
Your Blood *26*
Eternity Passion *29*
Witness *31*
Blessed Eyes *34*
Like Hinds' Feet *37*
Wisdom and Grace *40*
Clean *43*
Compassion *46*
The Quietude of Peace *48*
Transfixed *50*
Little/Alive *53*
Wherever You Are *56*
At the Same Place *58*
Stay *60*
At the Very Last Moment *63*
Rich Love *66*
Not to Harm *69*
Plea of a Broken Heart *72*

Build the Wall *75*
The Same Grace *78*
Dayspring of Power *81*
The Joy of Gladness *84*
A God Like Thunder *86*
Prepared *89*
Find You Here *92*
The Bread of Waiting *95*
Your Hand *98*
Atonement *100*
Revolution *102*
The Grace-filled Life *105*
Not What We Would Expect *108*
Enraptured in Your Love *111*
Priorities *113*

Preface

Our God is a God who does great things. He is a reconciler, a Father, and a friend. He has gifted me with a unique testimony that I would like to share with you. Everything He has done has been to His glory, and I would not be the same without His grace and the seasons of difficulty in my life.

His love truly makes us who we are. I grew up believing in a God who saves but primarily a God who judges, One who is ready to correct wrong and quick to punish us for our sin. Somewhere along the way, I missed the most important part, that God loves us. I did not understand what that truly meant until I was forced to come face to face with my fears and misconceptions and redefine for myself and my own faith who God really was and who He expects us to be.

The past is gone to God—forgiven. He cares about every new detail in every new day. He brings us to the same places where we have made mistakes before; this is not to harm us or punish us but to teach us and protect us. He is not a God who loves to harm. He is a God who loves His children with a transforming love, one that bears with us, patiently waiting, until we are completely sanctified each day, one decision at a time.

If we let him, God will show us the way in every step. God is so over-arching, encompassing, and completely perfect that there are no words to describe Him other than our Savior and our God. He has rescued us, and He will rescue you from all your fears and your failures. He will grow you in love, protect and shelter you, teach and refine you, if you trust in Him.

Just before I turned 30, God tested and tried me. He revealed the misconceptions about Him that lurked deep in my heart. He showed me how fully and entirely I could trust in Him. He revealed how relationships had crept into my life that had deceived me and made me compromise His Word just to believe that I was loved. He disclosed how we can only live one life in Him, and it must be an entirely devoted one. He taught me to become more aware of the desires that tugged at my heart and took me away from Him, the hope to please others first, the "need" to escape instead of submitting in obedience before Him. Most of all, He taught me that He is a sovereign God. What He says goes: He will bring it to pass. We will never actually lack anything when we trust completely in Him. He is the God who knows our needs and loves to provide.

God helped me experience that, yes, pain hurts, and sin hurts even more—it is so disruptive and alluring that there will never be a day on this earth when we are free of that fight. He alone provides the grace and strength to endure. He reminded me that we are children, no matter how old we get, and that He wants us to come to Him not only in times of need but in every time, when we are glad or anxious, when we are desperate or scared or don't know what to do. His Word stands also when He says in John 14:12-14 (NKJV), "'Most assuredly, I say to you, he who believes in Me, the works that I do he will do also; and greater works than these he will do, because I go to My Father. And whatever you ask in My name, that I will do, that the Father may be glorified in the Son. If you ask anything in My name, I will do it.'" This is the confidence our Father wants from us: a dependent relationship with Him based on need, centered in trust and love, that we would simply ask Him, and He would provide.

Another misinterpretation is that you must "earn" your way to faith, not by works per se, but that you have to earn God's favor once you are saved by doing all the "right" things. I knew God loved me and by His grace had saved me, but I compiled a mental checklist, a ritualized standard of living: go to church, pray, read the Bible enough, do what others ask, be humble and kind about serving—essentially, fill your life with enough God, and God will give you what you ask for. The truth is, we cannot fill ourselves with close to enough God to last us one moment in one day. Instead, it is the Holy Spirit who alone can fill us to overflowing, and it is only He who can give us the power of constancy to make a change and to keep and follow God's will. The most radical deviation from this world is living in obedience to God.

With Him, we can do the impossible. The Word is more than something you read to understand; it is spoken power, Living Water, and it brings life into our souls. We find ourselves in Him. God Himself is the Way, the Truth, and the Life. He cares about every single one of our hurts and concerns and every detail about us, yet He still loves us with the same grace as all His children. He cannot give to some and withhold from a few—He is not a changeable God—He does not withhold His love from anyone. He will, though, keep us in situations where we learn, often in difficult ways, until the proper time; the liberty that He gives us is obedience. This is not the liberty to do whatever we want but the liberty to follow Him, the ability to live free from the world and what it expects of us, the free gift to rely on our heavenly Creator and Father and know that despite what we see, He is the only truth, and He will provide. He never fails, and His answers always come at just the right time.

Friend, if you are considering right now whether you can follow God, know that you cannot do it alone, but when you trust in Him, His indwelling power will overflow you so much that you will know the real love of a Father and a friend. If you call out to Him, His Word promises that He will hear you from on high. "For 'whoever calls on the name of the Lord shall be saved,'" and, as it also says in Romans, "there is no partiality with God" (Romans 10:13, 2:11, NKJV). God is calling to you today: live in Him, walk in Him, and accept His perfect love for you, trusting that when you surrender, your life is in far better hands. We are commanded to love one another but also, first, to obey our God. You may consider praying the following to honor God and begin your walk with Christ.

> *Father God, please forgive me. I know that I have sinned and that nothing can take away Your love for me. I know that You are with me and for me always and even to the end.*
>
> *Please forgive me of my sins. I ask You to come into my life as Lord and Savior and make me clean. I acknowledge that You are on the throne and that Jesus Christ is the Son of God who died on the Cross for me.*
>
> *I know that He rose again to new life so that I could be with You and be saved. I acknowledge You personally as my Savior and Lord, God over all my life.*

I give You everything this day and will trust in You. Please open my eyes to see Your glory and make Your presence known in my life. In Jesus' name I pray. Amen!

The Lord has appeared of old to me, saying: "Yes, I have loved you with an everlasting love; Therefore with lovingkindness have I drawn you'" (Jeremiah 31:3, NKJV).

"For the law of the Spirit of life in Christ Jesus has made me free from the law of sin and death" (Romans 8:2, NKJV).

*And we know that the Son of God
has come and has given us an understanding,
that we may know Him who is true;
and we are in Him who is true,
in His Son Jesus Christ.
This is the true God
and eternal life.*

1 John 5:20, NKJV

 Alive

Oh, now is the hour, and let all the earth come alive in the glory of our Savior's majesty! For we are His instruments, growing memorials bearing testimony for our King, that each day we would gather in faith around Him and awake to exercise our hope! Let us remember His kindness, for He is always good, and hold fast to the truth, for He is faithful! There is no darkness in Him but only light and a heart for His people—God is never late, and He is always right on time.

Let us remember His fragrance, then, that restores and kindles our souls along with the cool breeze that carries relief for the weary. His whispers and the songs of life all about us commend His worthiness to us, for He is the beginning and end of all of our days. Surely, His provision is above every entity and ache of the heart, and there is no wound or break He cannot heal, no distance where He has not already made the way for a return. His Son, His Spirit who lives in us, witnesses our Father's careful grace. His longing yet is for restoration, bringing us to His arms again. There is no separation greater than that which Christ Himself has faithfully endured for our sake, no pain greater than being apart from Him. Because of Him only, we draw our breaths in freedom.

God waits on us patiently! He is the Lord, and He is gracious; He is Jesus, our Savior, and our God. For He is not immune to experiencing our troubles; He has known our pleasures and shared with us in our pain. Across every hill and valley, His Word calls to us, beckoning us to receive

Him in knowledge and truth! Even if we turn from Him, He is faithful, and His love covers every flaw. He forgives us, and His Spirit convicts us of sin and unrighteousness. His everlasting mercy is the reward of our hope! In Him alone can we overcome the darkness through the love of the Father that transforms our souls.

For we are surrounded by a myriad of distractions, and we are often weary; yet, let the trials of each day bring us back to Him in the end. Rather than covering the emptiness, let us come ready to be filled. God, root us and establish us in Your Word, which is the Bread of Life! For You make all things new, and these are the eyes of faith: to stand alone, God, to trust Your Word, to see with our souls (even when our hearts are broken) that Your glory is near! Even so, as we share with You in life, Jesus, we must also suffer with You in death, for we will be put to the test and refined in this world for a crown of glory that awaits us. Father, glorify Your name!

Let us look now to our Father who has given all on our behalf, in whom is every grace and provision, the confidence and promise of rest and of peace. He is the only One who can meet our needs perfectly. He is the Source, the Healer, the wellspring of life! He redeems us daily; He removes the burdens from our shoulders. In the coming days when His Spirit will be made known in a deeper way to those who believe, God, give us the perception to look with hope on the days that yet will come! Indeed, nothing is in Him that is allowed without cause. His intent for us remains fixed on our salvation. Even our highest hopes cannot measure against the immensity of His plans, and the love and abundance He desires for us to behold! For it is in being refined that we are defined, and in suffering when we must move forward to a stronger hope than we alone can lay hold of. Oh, let us delight in Him once more, for joyful restoration, for peace, and for forgiveness! We are created for the purpose of redemption to abide in His love.

> *It came about the same night that the word of God came to Nathan, saying, "Go and tell David My servant, 'Thus says the Lord, "You shall not build a house for Me to dwell in; for I have not dwelt in a house since the day I brought up Israel to this day, but I have gone from tent to tent and from one dwelling place to another. In all places where I have walked with all Israel, have I spoken a word with any of the judges of Israel, whom I commanded to shepherd My people, saying, 'Why have you not built for Me a house of cedar?'" Now, therefore, thus shall you say to My servant David, 'Thus says the Lord of hosts, "I took you from the pasture, from following the sheep, to be leader over My people Israel. I have been with you wherever you have gone, and have cut off all your enemies from before you; and I will make you a name like the name of the great ones who are in the earth. I will appoint a place for My people Israel, and will plant them, so that they may dwell in their own place and not be moved again; and the wicked will not waste them anymore as formerly..."'"* (1 Chronicles 17:3-9, NASB).

True God

～ The Brokenness of Creation ～

O Lord, how Your body was pierced and torn for us, Your blood poured out to bring us life! The bitter cup of salvation, which is all of pain and sin itself, You patiently drank for us. Jesus, we rejoice in Your sinless love! You are the Good Shepherd, who has laid down Your life for Your sheep. You put Your precious and unfailing love on display for us, so that we who are helpless may be restored once more! For a long time we have fought to be free, but our best efforts can never free ourselves; now, with the battle won, we yield in surrender to You.

O Lord, we come before You, and we witness the truth! For You live, and You are for us. Even Your power to resurrect Your Son from the grave has been poured into our hearts, for we are new creations and Your everlasting testimony lives within us, our God! Though we may never know tomorrow, still Your grace is more than enough in every hour. Jesus, Your promises are our strength! From gladness to sorrow, still we will praise You. To the measure of all our days, let Your glory come forth and shine through us! You, who are of eternity, do not falter. Let us stand in You, O God, in faith, with hope and love! Reach down and save us, Father, for it is apart from You that we are blinded. Help us to fear You, knowing the pressing power of Your will to save! Let us perceive Your glory as You fill us to overflowing with Your love.

When all else fades, then everything left is Yours. In You alone is every resource and power in heaven and on earth to transform us, that we would be made whole again!

What endures is not our strength, but the hope You place inside us, which is ever strong in You. Oh, Father, You are our Rock and our defender, our shield and refuge in the storm! You came; You call even now to us. You will certainly rescue us from the darkness, for You and You alone have overcome! Open our eyes, O Lord, to save us; save us, that we may rejoice in You again!

For though You had all authority under heaven, You forbore the suffering for our sake. O Lord, You chose to endure out of love for us, to be a faithful witness. You came that the new covenant would be established, perfecting the Law by grace, for only You can satisfy. With humble hearts, let us come before You, Jesus, as heirs and servants. Let us repent and acknowledge the works of our God!

> *It is He who made the earth by His power, who established the world by His wisdom; and by His understanding, He has stretched out the heavens...the portion of Jacob is not like these; for the Maker of all is He, and Israel is the tribe of His inheritance; the Lord of hosts is His name. Pick up your bundle from the ground, you who dwell under siege! For thus says the Lord, "Behold I am slinging out the inhabitants of the land at this time, and will cause them distress, that they may be found"...I know, O Lord, that a man's way is not in himself, nor is it in a man who walks to determine his steps. Correct me, O Lord, but with justice; not with Your anger, or You will bring me to nothing* (Jeremiah 10:12, 16-18, 23-24, NASB).

God to the Full

O Lord, how great You are! Your love reaches to the heavens, Your mercies to the skies! You abound in lovingkindness, for You are the oil of gladness and the garment of praise. How perfect is Your blessed Law for restoration, our Savior! You are the light that shines in the darkness and makes broken men complete.

Though we cannot comprehend Your ways, still, Father, our trust takes hold in You. You are infinite and Your goodness endures forever, for You are the God of all Creation who formed us, the Author of our lives from beginning to end. Now, we lay our lives before You, Father, the sacrifice of thanksgiving and praise, for You hold our hearts. You jealously guard those You love, Lord God, and even Your Son tenderly keeps us sheep within His fold.

Freedom is before those who seek You, and those who follow You to the end of their days will be blessed. Your authority works miracles within us! You heal the hurting, Lord God, and You establish us, so let our foremost cry be to worship You alone! Oh, Father, for not a single act is outside Your sovereignty, but You are working it all to Your purposes for good; neither is anyone lost to Your mercy, for Your grace surpasses all measure and reason. You are the peace within the storm. We trust in You: let us come to know You. Father, we pray that we may dwell in the fullness of Your holiness that we would value Your faithfulness above all! Jesus, You are the delight of our souls and our comfort. Strengthen us, O Lord, against time.

Every season, You allow for our good and for our

learning and growth within You. You bring new life and a new covenant to displace the old. In the stillness, in the silence, we rest in You. Teach us, O Lord, as You have molded us into new creations! Your voice is a whisper, directing the way ahead in wisdom; teach us to discern by Your Spirit the paths of Your unfailing Word! Your fruitfulness rises up within us as we obey You, for You cannot be quenched! Surely we are Your people, and You have formed us that we may know You. You have come to save us, Lord Jesus, that we may be one with You again, for You alone endure.

Father, now, let us bow to receive You, for there is no trial too great or small to submit to You; You hearken to us in our humility as we return before Your throne. You are gentle to those who are meek; Your love is patient and kind; Your ears are attentive to us. Oh, Lord, we rejoice, for You have delivered us—draw us near, do not let us go! For our names are written on Your heart, and surely You have known us every day. With undeserved grace You defend us! Let us rest securely in faith and attentiveness, knowing Your victory is won! Bless us, O Lord, and show us mercy, and let us walk in Your way in confidence, for You are our God!

> *And the Lord said to Abram, after Lot had separated from him, "Lift up your eyes now and look from the place where you are...for all the land which you see I give to you and your descendants forever. And I will make your descendants as the dust of the earth; so that if a man could number the dust of the earth, then your descendants also could be numbered. Arise, walk in the*

land through its length and its width; for I give it to you." Then Abram moved his tent, and went and dwelt by the terebinth trees of Mamre, which are in Hebron, and built an altar there to the Lord (Genesis 13:14-18, NKJV).

 Greatest Praise

O Lord, the greatest sacrifice we could offer You is that of our thanksgiving and our praise. Even in our brokenness, still You are faithful, and we bring sincere hearts before Your throne. We worship You, Jesus, as we bring the submission of trust and praise. With hands lifted high and voices raised to exalt the works of Your hands, let us thank You, our Lord! For all wisdom and grace and understanding is Yours and all power—these were with You before the world began—You have given us Your Word, that we may seek You, and You will instruct us all the day. Surely, You are the Counselor of the heavens, our perfect Judge and Creator, God. You have loved Your children before there was yet one of us, in Your mercy and kindness, O Lord!

We know that You can do miracles: You took the universe from space and You formed us from dust in Your hands; You breathed Your life into us, shaped us in Your image and given us Your heart. Again, Father, let us fall to our knees to serve You, in awe at how gracious You are. In the deserts and rain, in the fire and through the wind and storm, You have never left our side—Your love and forgiveness endures, O God.

You open the expanse before us, permitting us to run in broad spaces that we may not stumble; You level the mountains that we may walk up them from the valley, where Your Word has humbled us. You build paths before us and establish our steps in Your faithfulness; we are justified in You! Though we are afflicted, however, now You have given us the desire of our heart. All our hope is in You, God; there is no love so great as that which You have given us, that You have restored us by Your perfect sacrifice! Our anxieties are not from You but from the enemy who would have us doubt Your goodness. Your plans for us, Father, preserve against the test of time.

Lord, You favor us in Your love who seek You; You created life for us to discover and explore. You root us to grow, and You uproot us to find You and seek You where we once before were lacking. Now, in the silence, we hear You calling, and You draw us to Your Word. You call to us in compassion, for there is none like You. Surely, we will be known by our faith in surrender, our hope and trust in God who alone holds the strength to restore. For You are perfect, and You make us like You, Jesus, for You are crowned with glory, and now victory waits at the gates for those who endure. Let us not be ashamed who wait upon You, Jesus, but show us Your confident end, that we may rejoice in Your love.

When we go deeper into Your Word, Lord, then we receive our sight. You are for us and not against us, and Your justice works wonders in Your love. You hear our every prayer and surpass every expectation of our uncertain plans. You alone have passed through both heaven and hell for Your people, and You search the hearts of men. Even when we cannot perceive it, still You are working Your witness, and Your glory will be revealed. The sacrifice that is most pleasing to You, God, is the garment of humility with praise, and Your Word is the true witness.

Surely You will deliver and restore us, opening the springs about us and filling us with the goodness of Your heart! Your Spirit reveals to us the darkness, that we would be laid bare to Your power and changed by Your hand, for there is no length to which You would not go to save us, our Father and our God!

> *"Then this shall be a sign for you: you shall eat this year such as grows of itself, and in the second year what springs from the same; also in the third year sow and reap, plant vineyards and eat the fruit of them. And the remnant who have escaped of the house of Judah shall again take root downward, and bear fruit upward. For out of Jerusalem shall go a remnant, and those who escape from Mount Zion. The zeal of the Lord of hosts will do this." Therefore thus says the Lord concerning the king of Assyria: "He shall not come into this city, nor shoot an arrow there, nor come before it with a shield, nor build a siege mound against it. By the way that he came, by the same he shall return; and he shall not come into this city," says the Lord. "For I will defend this city, to save it for My own sake and for My servant David's sake"* (2 Kings 19:29-34, NKJV).

The Cross Too Heavy to Bear

Awake, all you who seek the Lord, for now is the time when we are pressed. What cross is too heavy to bear when we consider the sacrifice of our Savior? He who took the burden and shame for our every sin carries us still. Our Lord is worthy, faithful to be trusted and deserving of all praise. Who can be condemned who follows Him, who has risen with Him from the grave into new life? He was subject to every insult and reviling, all penalty on our behalf, and yet we doubted. How permanent was His deliverance for us then, and how enduring His rescue now! When we are persecuted, then He considers us blessed. There is no trouble He has not experienced, no trial that we would endure where He has not first paved the way. Our God overcomes, and He who has known our afflictions remembers them. He is tender and compassionate to His people, so that we do not journey alone.

For our enemy stalks about in darkness, but our God calms the raging sea; He commands deliverance by faith: one word from Him is enough! For ours is the God who offers peace to those who thirst for righteousness, and those whom He gives over to disobedience, He does so only for a time that they may be found. He who laid down His life for us surely will not let us waste away, but His love eagerly pursues: He always provides at the perfect time. Let us obtain abundance, yet in the same faithful trust which He has also shown us in relation to the Father, receive the restoration that only He can provide. Though we stumble, let us never depart from His Word.

If we are rejected, then, for the sake of His truth, let us be comforted, for the Lord exalts the humble. All praise and glory be to Him, who makes all things new! He works wonders in the depths of the unseen and discloses the human heart. He is the everlasting hope, and He gives us strength by His Word to complete what He has begun. Indeed, for the light suffering we endure is a crown to our benefit, bearing the hallmark of His love. Our beauty on the outside is passing, but rooted love grows within and stays grounded, yes, and the house of the Lord will stand! So let us awaken, O people of God, to be received by our Father; let us submit in obedience, with reverence to our King!

For we live in a world of injustice but one which our God has overcome. There is no satisfaction without Him, no other rescue from our own sin than by the Cross. Let us live then for His glory, all those who are freed in Him. He answers His people in faithfulness and truth!

At the perfect time in Your unfailing plan, You come for us and receive us into the everlasting, for this is our affirmation. You are the hope that does not fade, the way of fruitfulness that does not wither, and You are the forgiveness that never fails us, O Lord, our Savior, our God!

> *Those who sat in darkness and in the shadow of death, bound in affliction and irons—because they rebelled against the words of God, and despised the counsel of the Most High, therefore He brought down their heart with labor; they fell down, and there was none to help. Then they cried out to the Lord in their trouble, and He saved them out of their distresses. He brought them out dark-*

ness and the shadow of death, and broke their chains in pieces. Oh, that men would give thanks to the Lord for His goodness, and for His wonderful works to the children of men! For He has broken the gates of bronze, and cut the bars of iron in two (Psalm 107:10-16, NKJV).

 The Separation Divide

Oh, Lord, You have borne what we never could: separation from the Father, for no matter for how short a time. You passed through the shade of sin and death to bring us new life. You conquered the divide between us and have taken our place, that we would rise in the light of Your glory, the saving power of our God! No grief could ever come close to the price You paid for us. In love, You who are flawless, the unblemished Lamb, laid down Your own life. Jesus, You endured the greatest of terrors for our sake, for our deliverance, that iniquity would overpower us no more.

For in You, Lord, we are freed from the law of sin and death; we are taken out of darkness by Your compassion into a reborn life, resurrection in You eternally. In this world, we are Your emissaries, and Your light is within us, Your Spirit abiding in us. We wait eagerly for the unfolding of Your Word, our God! There is no life apart from You, no covering greater than the sacrifice of Your blood which has covered all our sins; so also there is nothing that can exceed the measure of Your grace for us. No might can stand against those who make You their refuge; we trust in You in all of our days, for You are our everlasting strength; You are faithful, O God.

Your people are before You, Lord; hearken to us, and let our cries be heard in Your holy place! Answer us, Father, from the depths of our souls where we are hurting most. Establish victory, plant in our hearts the new name You have promised us as Your children, and lead us into the inheritance You have prepared! We take up our cross; pour out Your compassion upon us and let the oil of anointing flow, knowing that we are found in You, and Your presence is forever, for we will have confidence in You! Let us be led forth in faith for Your kingdom, Jesus; cover us with Your truth, that we may begin again.

For Your calling upon us is for life, God! Here we learn the dependency to trust and lean upon You, assured that You will save. Yet once more, with the smallest seed of faith and hope in You, You yield the greatest harvest. Let us make ready the paths for our Lord! In You alone, there is a shelter for Your people, for You do not despise the brokenhearted, our God. You baptize with fire, Jesus, and You cleanse with rain. You purge and cleanse and refine the hearts that are claimed for Your kingdom, and surely, You will deliver us! Save us, Father, from despair, for You have grown us and given us power and authority, the keys to enter Your kingdom. We hold fast to You as we cling to Your side! There is no one besides You, and no one more faithful, God Most High!

> *I descended to the roots of the mountains. The earth with its bars was around me forever, but You have brought up my life from the pit, O Lord my God. While I was fainting away, I remembered the Lord, and my prayer came to You, into Your holy temple. Those who regard vain idols forsake their faithfulness, but I will sacrifice to You with the voice of thanksgiving. That which I have vowed I will pay. Salvation is from the Lord." Then the Lord commanded the fish, and it vomited Jonah up onto the dry land* (Jonah 2:6-10, NASB).

When You Paint the Stars

When You paint the stars, O God, Your creation endures until the appointed time, when another light takes its place. You fill the expanse with Your love and tenderness for Your people; Your faithfulness remains as a testimony long after the first is gone. Your care and compassion govern us, Jesus, and all Your ways are good, bathed in the glory and richness of hope for a future. In every circumstance, You shepherd us, keeping us safe as we submit to You. We look unto the heavens and up to the Cross where we see You; we behold Your majesty and remember the strength and beauty of Your sacrifice and Your plan. Surely, You clothe us gently in Your wisdom, in mercy and grace even despite our failures. You always provide, that we would never be too far gone. Only because of You, Jesus, only in Your love shall we stand!

What holiness is Yours, Father, You who existed and were worthy to be exalted before time began. You called out the light and flooded the nations; You decreed, and the earth was formed. You know all our paths, and there is no end to Your greatness, for who can hide from You? You know all the corners of our broken hearts, for You are mighty, and You are refining us, that we would declare the sovereignty of Your perfect will! Even above our doubts and fears, You are with us, and You never leave us, O God.

Your Holy Spirit speaks confidence into our souls, for You are our matchless guide; we are nothing when compared with Your power, which is limitless, but in Your love, daily, You rescue us! You know all the details and have woven them intricately into Your plan, for You crafted us as instruments with hearts and hands for service to bring You praise and glory. Oh, for You are the life within us and the purpose of our every breath—to live for You, Jesus, to tell of Your works, and to share in Your love! You alone have delivered us, and You alone restore.

You made us to dwell in perfect peace with You, Father, in harmony to exalt You, to occupy us in fruitful pursuits and wonders that bring You joy and glory. Even our souls arise to meet You, our saving God! We pray, encourage us to obedience that we may remain steadfast in You, for not from vindictiveness but in mercy and a Father's love do You pierce hearts according to Your purpose! God, You clothe us with splendor, that we may be seen and known by You, a true reflection to the world around us as we witness, abiding in hope and trusting in You alone!

For hope reigns in You, Father, an impossible love where mercy and justice collide. You are powerful, You are our Savior, and You are our sufficiency, O God! You hearken to our desperate pleas; You are patient but have an appointed time and call. You are Light and worthy and working all about us, our defender! You touch us, and we are changed. Oh, even now, as in every moment, consider us, and conform us to You, for You bear our cares upon Your shoulders. Your willing salvation towards us is more than we can understand.

You are faithful and just, true and holy, and how great is Your majesty! You move mountains when we pray; barren lands break forth into springs before You, so deep is Your grace that You have covered our every sin in love! For as sheep who were lost and wandering, now we know our

Shepherd, and You have stamped us with the mark of grace among Your flock. You will not lose one whom Your Father has entrusted You with, for there is none like You, our God! You pursue and sustain Your children. Let us shine across the distance boldly, that even after we are gone, our lives would glorify You, our good and faithful King!

> *And Mary said, "My soul exalts the Lord, and my spirit has rejoiced in God my Savior. For He has regard for the humble state of His bondslave; for behold, from this time on all generations will count me blessed. For the Mighty One has done great things for me; and holy is name. And His mercy is upon generation after generation toward those who fear Him. He has done mighty deeds with His arm; He has scattered those who were proud...He has brought down rulers from their thrones, and has exalted those who were humble. He has filled the hungry with good things...He has given help to Israel His servant, in remembrance of His mercy..."*
> (Luke 1:46-54, NASB).

⁓ Who Will Turn Back ⁓

What a beautiful day You have given us, O Lord, a day rich with possibilities and new in hope—You are gracious and kind! God, let us entrust each of our steps to You this day, for You are able; You are faithful; and we delight in You. Lead us in wisdom, we pray, that we will hear Your voice and listen, that we would return to You as one body, made new and complete in Your plan.

When we follow You, then surely we are blessed, for there is nothing good that You would withhold from us, no mercies You would not give when we call out to You. Help us, O Lord, to cease striving and know You, to live in the confidence that You love us, knowing You are in us and for us, and You are at work in everything. If we boast in anything, let it be of this, that You are mighty, that we have seen and known Your goodness and tasted Your mercy, that You have revealed Your heart. We seek You only, God, and the comfort and strength of Your hand to glorify Your name, as one in faith with You—let us testify! There is no trial we experience that is greater than what You have already overcome. You allow testing to refine us, but Your endurance and mercy never fail in Your perfect love. You are the God of the Heavens, the God of all time—everywhere we look, we behold You. Jesus, give us eyes to see and serve, to reflect You faithfully, O God!

You are so mindful of our weaknesses, the ease with which we stumble, and the fragile condition of our hearts; let us surrender to Your Spirit, that You would take control. You consider us in inestimable grace who seek You, and

You know just how we can manage and the strength we need. For You have weighed the cost of our salvation and found its value beyond gold; we are priceless to You, God! We pray, and Your answer comes before us; we weep, and Your power is near to save. For the sake of Your kingdom and the sake of Your glory, Almighty God, we worship and beseech You with praise and thanksgiving: uplift us, deliver us, our God! Draw us to Yourself, for we are empty, and fill us with Your wisdom, Father, Your unending love!

Let us hold fast to You, for Your Word is certain; Your promises do not fail! When we cry out for mercy and knowledge, You hear us, and we are found by You. For You are all around us, working as Your Spirit moves—it is like a mighty stream that floods our souls, proclaiming truth and righteousness. Father, speak to us swiftly, for we long to do Your will! The poor in spirit shall find their refuge in You, and our hunger and thirst will be satisfied. You do not bruise the broken, but You heal us—our weakness abounds, but Your strength is more. Teach us to know Your voice and follow You without hesitation, our Redeemer, that we may walk in Your ways.

For You have laid Your life down for us, and who will You find worthy? For we are just men, but so also we give You our all, that You would fill us with Your Spirit, Lord Jesus, to dwell within us so that we may accomplish the impossible by faith in Your glorious name! For though we have been strictly chastened and humbled, now is the harvest time. In Your peace and decision, You have secured victory for us, the light of our salvation and our souls forever, O God! Your love and grace endure forever, Your faithfulness to the end of time!

Then King David went in and sat before the Lord, and he said, "Who am I, O Lord God? And what is my house, that You brought me this far? And yet this was a small thing in Your sight, O Lord God, and You have also spoken of Your servant's house for a great while to come. Is this the manner of man, O Lord God? Now what more can David say to You? For You, Lord God, know Your servant. For Your word's sake, and according to Your own heart, You have done all these great things, to make Your servant know them. Therefore You are great, O Lord God. For there is none like You, nor is there any God besides You, according to all that we have heard with our ears" (2 Samuel 7:18-22, NKJV).

Open and Free

Open the doors, O Lord, and may Your glory enter this place, for Your Gospel exalts Your majesty and pierces our hearts with truth! Hear the voice of our supplications, Father, and answer us with Your saving right hand. In conviction and righteousness, grace and mercy, You are the breath of life! For today is a day of victory, of triumph against the dark, of a new song that is sung before You, giving passionate praise, our God! Yours is the sword that has divided us, separating the spirit from the flesh; also, Yours is the love that transforms and heals us, for all power under heaven and on earth is Yours, our King! As we live our days with choices made in love to demonstrate Your care, Father, so let us walk into Your purposes, bearing Your Cross, living Your testimony, as we submit to You.

Open our hearts, that You would freely flood this place; open the doors that we may be filled and raised to new life by Your overarching love! Your compassion never fails us, giving us a glimpse of what is to come—new hope, a radiant new life filled with creation. Let us trust wholeheartedly in You! Let us fall before You humbly and in service, exchanging our pride for Your strength—for Yours is all authority, Father, and You make us to stand. You are perfect and just, and Your Word cannot be undone. Your commands are decreed for faith and for good purposes; teach us Your heart, and show us Your mercy!

For Your way is progress, where doubt succumbs to the promises of Your Word. You long to embrace and draw us near. Your blessings abound, and You are peace and protection, strength and confidence when we obey You. You ask not for flawlessness but for sincere hearts with confession and repentance, ready to be remade by You. Surely, for You have given us a new name in this day and appointed us once more; no longer are we abandoned, for You have never forsaken us. You have chosen us while yet we were Your enemies.

Let us give thanks to our God! Let us commune with You just as we are, humbled and broken but restored to reawakened life. Let us never fear to ask freely, for this pleases You, O Lord. You have delivered us from all our fears. You never fail to comfort us when we acknowledge our failures—You forever forgive us as when we turn to You. Your love shines within us, for by Your hand alone we have been rescued, and in Your love and faithfulness, You have confirmed us. Surely, You establish us as Your own. You are the God of justice and of patient kindness to those who know You, a God of perfect grace, power, and peace. We come to You, prepared with tender hearts to be healed, for You reign victorious, and You have refined us. Father, for only You make us whole again.

> *And He said to them, "Can you make the friends of the bridegroom fast while the bridegroom is with them? But the days will come when the bridegroom will be taken away from them; then they will fast in those days." Then He spoke a parable to them: "No one puts a piece from a new garment on an old one; otherwise the new makes a tear, and also the piece that was taken out of the new does not match the old. And no one puts new wine into old wineskins; or else the new wine will burst*

the wineskins and be spilled, and the wineskins will be ruined. But new wine must be put into new wineskins, and both are preserved" (Luke 5:34-38, NKJV).

Your Blood

O God, You have deemed us so precious that You gave Your only begotten Son for us, the perfect spotless Lamb. You spoke light into the world, and You are the Living Word. You have gone to prepare a place that we may dwell with You always, Lord, near to Your perfect throne. Your grace is more than enough as is Your obedience and sacrifice, Your perfect love which covers every flaw. Our intercessor, You are He who cares for us, our Shepherd, our Savior, and our God!

Forgive us, Jesus, for our trespasses and iniquities are without number; yet You are faithful, and You transform our hearts and spirits with all power necessary to overcome. By Your Spirit, Lord, You love us as children, heirs who are growing in character and strength. You love us patiently with endless grace, and where once we were devoid of understanding, now we hunger and thirst for You, God! You have blessed us—even Your chastening has been a mercy, Father, opening our spirits to see Your true nature. You have shown us who You are and magnified Yourself in our failures, that You are mighty and victorious—You forgive! Help us, Father, to remember always that, in an unsteady world, You are our security.

Oh, our Father, let us rejoice in You, for Your joy is not temporal; it is lasting, of an eternal love and hope which springs from Your faithful heart! Even a glimpse of Your presence, one word of Your comfort is enough to sustain us; Your grace overshadows our weakness, imbuing us with strength! Unify our hearts to seek You, Father; may all the walls fall that we may once more rebuild upon Your Word according to all You command. Hear our prayers and establish us, for You are our peace and sure salvation; ignite us with Your conviction, heal us and bind us together, we pray. Bring us gently into Your tabernacle, Father—yes, for You take us by the hand.

Forgive us, our Lord—we will praise You! Have mercy on us, Father, that we may endure. You are clothed in light and rich in majesty; we who follow You stand protected and preserved—we trust You, O God. For the sake of the glory of Your name, You relentlessly pursue us; purify us to seek You and conform our faces to the image of Your Son! For the sake of Your power and Your unchangeable Word, Lord, redeem those who look to You in the pillar of light, the cloud and fire in the midst of darkness. You will guide us to the end—we surrender our hearts to You!

Your Word illuminates our steps; Your wisdom and goodness beckon to us. God, help us to remain true to Your statutes, zealous and eager to feast on Your all-providing love! O Lord, You are with us and for us; Your Word is true and faithful, and You hold our sorrows close to Your heart. Let us then be holy as You are holy; oh, let us repent and be broken and fill us with Your love once more, Lord Jesus! Teach us, Father, with a vision to live in Your purpose; establish the work of our hands; yes, and establish us, that we may have joy in You, our Lord!

For You, O Lord of hosts, God of Israel, have revealed this to Your servant, saying, "I will build you a house." Therefore Your servant has found it in his heart to pray this prayer to You. And now, O Lord God, You are God, and Your words are true, and You have promised this goodness to Your servant. Now therefore, let it please You to bless the house of Your servant, that it may continue before You forever; for you, O Lord God, have spoken it, and with Your blessing let the house of Your servant be blessed forever (2 Samuel 7:27-29, NKJV).

Eternity Passion

O God, Your eternity encompasses us, Your grace surrounds us. You have created and acted in faithfulness from the beginning to the end, and every second is within Your loving hands of mercy. We are persecuted and misunderstood, and we who follow You encounter every kind of trial; yet we remember that all we do is for You, O Lord, and so we endure, knowing it is but a small sacrifice compared to what You have done. We are repaid evil for good, even by those who love us, yet, at the finish, still our hope stands. Though we suffer, You are with us—You will not let us fall. You are the Judge and the covenant between us; You are faithful to forgive.

O Lord Jesus, there is no greater love than to lay down one's life down for their friends, and this is what You have done for us. You have conquered death itself—what a beautiful existence to be found in You! You are Alpha and Omega, He who makes all things new; You are our Savior and sovereign God who heals us, our Redeemer in every time. Though we are rejected on this earth because of You, You make a place for us in the skies. When the earth itself shakes and falters, still we are found in You. You keep us in wisdom and guard us in peace, God; firm in Your foundation, we rest in Your love. You uplift our heads and preserve us, for You are the courage and strength within our hearts, the wisdom and faith that keeps us our eyes searching for You, waiting for Your glorious day. Surely, our home is in heaven with You, to be beside You for all eternity.

God, in the harrowing seasons and trials, it is the vision

of You that keeps us alive. You purify us and chasten us in love until all we know is Your Word. Even when we say we can take no more, Your calling does not waver. You, who are our lasting hope, never become unsettled or run short of grace. Jesus—You are our morning star! You encircle closely about us and are the fulfillment of every prophecy, the sure witness that our Father is true. Your mercy abounds, and all that You have spoken, You will surely perform. Earnestly we wait upon Your name and victory—oh, restore our lives, Lord God! Save and deliver us, for You meet us and hold us just where we are.

> *"The God of Israel said, The Rock of Israel spoke to me, 'He who rules over men righteously, who rules in the fear of God is as the light of the morning when the sun rises, a morning without clouds, when the tender grass springs out of the earth, through sunshine after rain.' Truly is not my house so with God? For He has made an everlasting covenant with me, ordered in all things, and secured. For all my salvation and all my desire; will He not indeed make it grow?"* (2 Samuel 23:3-5, NASB).

 Witness

O Lord, You humble us just at the right moment; let our sensitivity to Your Spirit increase as our soul draws near to You. In every circumstance, we are reminded of Your absolute sovereignty; for it is not we who succeed but You, Lord Jesus, and Your grace within us working for our good and Your glory. You desire fullness of joy for us, Father, praise at the witness of all You have done; only by faithful obedience and rest in You can we be completely satisfied! Though the flesh grows weak, still in You we are able—surely, we stand in Your Word, Lord God, and You are always with us! We trust in You and abide in the shelter of Your wisdom; even in the midst of trial, You are faithful, Jesus, our Savior whom we serve.

You enfold us in Your love and majesty all around us, revealing exactly what we need to know. You keep us safe, as You are our refuge—You love us and never leave us without You! You will not permit those who seek You to be greatly moved; You bring us to our knees to acknowledge Your greatness, and though we wrestle with forces greater than we can comprehend, Your grace has set us free, You have already conquered; the end is Yours, O God! You give peace and everlasting confidence to Your children; You permit every aspect of the gifts which You have given us to grow in to genuine fruitfulness to glorify You—we cannot escape from Your Word! Let us recall, now in this age to love one another, that we are separate from this world.

Help us understand that Your love, Lord, transcends every circumstance, time, and order; You work through us, with us, and for us to magnify Your holy name! Surely, You are wonderful, Jesus, for to rely on You is a blessing and resolute assurance; to turn to You in decision is a faithful surrender and not a harm. Oh, Lord Jesus, as You call us out to come to You, calm the tempest of insecurities about us; encourage us to stand! Comfort us in our afflictions, Father, that we may see and serve You in the storm. You are gracious and merciful, and what You plan and desire is always best. Your faithfulness is an immovable foundation—Your Word is more powerful than we can understand.

Father, Your Spirit is conviction and mighty counsel for Your people; how gracious You are, our Savior, for we find You always in perfect readiness in all seasons. Your greatness and righteousness pursue us, Your purposes for redemption and forgiveness do not fail! Lead us, O Lord, into a deeper, true understanding of You! Your heart is faithful, ready to confirm and provide strength; Your light shines in the darkness; and Your Spirit directs us, even those who are wounded and weak. For there is no burden You would not bear, no circumstance You will not use to prove Your love to us, Father, that all Your promises are true forever, as is the Word of Your Son! You alone are the Author of our Salvation, and You know our place. Now, Jesus, let us come before You in victory and with the sacrifice of thanksgiving, in awe of all You have done.

> *For, on the one hand, there is an annulling of the former commandment because of its weakness and unprofitableness, for the Law made nothing perfect; on the other hand, there is the bringing in of a better hope, through which we draw near to God. And inasmuch as*

He was not made priest without an oath (for they have become priests without an oath, but He with an oath by Him who said to Him: "The Lord has sworn and will not relent, 'You are a priest forever according to the order of Melchizedek'), by so much more Jesus has become the surety of a better covenant...therefore He also is able to save to the uttermost those who come to God through Him, since He always lives to make intercession for them" (Hebrews 7:18-22, 25, NKJV).

~ Blessed Eyes ~

Give thanks to the Lord, and never give up hope, for He is with us always. In the secret mercies, in the deep corners of our hearts, His true and holy Spirit knows us, and we relinquish all our fears to Him! For our God is our provider; He illumines our paths when we walk justly and uprightly in Him. He is our refuge and our strength, the only One who can bring abundance—surely, His faithfulness is always at work! Though so often we cannot reconcile His ways or the design of His purpose in accordance with His will, yet all of our troubles rest before Him. It is only by His grace and sacrifice that we hope—and are certain—to attain all that is good.

Though we cannot see His Word, in every moment, it stands; it is active and alive, the very foundation of our hearts. For our God's love remains, and He is merciful; His victory is already completed for us—we are safe and held secure in His hand. God is infinite; He loves us, and He is sovereign. There is no despising Him nor is there any shame for those who walk in Him, for He has paid it all! His paths are incomparable, and all His promises are true which are being revealed in us. He establishes us that we rise to everlasting strength in Him. We are victors in Christ, warriors who have already withstood the fight, that all the world may know His testimony, that every knee will bow to make His glory made known among men!

In our contentment with Him, then we have real life! In the eternal, even in the present, His reward is being with Him, and He comes quickly to save. For our troubles are temporary and passing and for so short a time; yet, He endures forever and His storehouses are full for us—He prepares them to overflow! For as our God has heard us from the beginning, He descends now with a shout. He walks in compassion yet shines His might and power through us, for He is worthy of all praise! In humbleness of heart, there do we find our Savior, and in recollected peace, He makes us whole: our first love, our Father, our sanctified life in Him!

Take heed then, to His commands, and let us faithfully serve the Lord; seek Him all the day, pray in trial, rejoice even in the midst of the storm! For He is faithful, ready to forgive and able; He is just, and all of His people will abide in Him. Let us prepare and be mindful to obey—His grace and salvation are near, ready to purge the darkness, returning His people to life! For wisdom belongs to him who asks for it, and our God freely gives and restores; indeed, let the mountains be shaken, for the day of the Lord draws near! Fear God, then, for in the day the walls fall, He will be our rescue. Even now His power pours from the clouds and echoes His majesty, exalting the weak and bringing the proud low, that all would glorify and rejoice in His great name! His faithfulness carries into each day with a persistence like the dawn; His lovingkindness meets us in the morning and renews us. He is compassionate and gracious, mindful that we are but men. Oh, Father, we give thanks to You unceasingly, for the time has come, and even now, Your hand is working wonders, transforming and conforming us to the image of Your beloved Son.

After these things Jesus walked in Galilee; for He did not want to walk in Judea, because the Jews sought to kill Him. Now the Jews' Feast of Tabernacles was at hand. His brothers therefore said to Him, "Depart from here and go into Judea, that Your disciples also may see the works that You are doing. For no one does anything in secret while he himself wishes to be known openly. If you do these things, show Yourself to the world." For even His brothers did not believe in Him. Then Jesus said to them, "My time has not yet come, but your time is always ready" (John 7:1-6, NKJV).

≈ Like Hinds' Feet ≈

Father, we return to You—at this precipice, we call out upon Your name! For Your Son, Jesus Christ, is the only way to freedom, that justice may be accomplished in You. You are the God of miracles, and He is the light! His Spirit leads us and guides us as a shepherd who guards His flock all throughout the night and day, for You have broken the chains of fear and shame, and in You is victory!

You were humbled, Lord, as we have never been; at the Cross, You gave Your life willingly for us, a blameless sacrifice, that we may live! You are the everlasting atonement; Your law and Your heart for redemption is greater than any pain. You have died for our freedom, that the power of Your resurrection may rest on us, and in You is the perfect fulfillment of the Father's plan. You have partaken of our every experience, every brokenness and sorrow, that You may minister to us in Your saving and unfailing grace and perfect love, O Lord. You have known our joy and our failures, for You came to sanctify and cleanse us, to know us as Your own. You hear our every plea, God; no more let us refuse Your commands and Your compassion, O God, for Your mercy is sufficient for every time and need. The depths of Your wisdom are only surpassed by Your love.

Father, let us remember with thankful hearts that Your call upon us is everlasting; let us go out courageously in boldness and truth for Your Word! Your eye is upon Your people, and Your Spirit searches us out; now, we pray, protect and keep us—our Shepherd, our Savior, and our God! In the wilderness, in the times when we cannot see or are rejected, You are with us all the more. Open the doorways to Your justice and majesty, and lay Your paths of peace before us, Father, for we are Your servants, and we hunger and thirst for You!

Though we grow tired, yet still the joy of our redemption stands. You are compassionate, the light which cannot be put out—You have torn down, and You shall mend up, O God. You are so mighty that every word You have spoken is proven true; You will surely look upon Your people again with kindness and mercy, to build up and no more tear down. For Lord, in You, even in this day, the past is forgotten; You give us new eyes to witness life spring forth! You revive us, who trust in You, that we would turn to You always and be forgiven forever, knowing we are completely saved. Your promises are for eternity, our God!

For while the paths of darkness are wide and inviting, cloaked in sin and death, Father, Your grace is more! Your Son came to set us free, to ransom us back from the grave and to redeem us. His Spirit convicts us, that we may embrace all we have in You. Only You can reveal Your purposes in Your perfect love. Let us be blinded no more but take root in You, Jesus, growing steadfastly and in fruitfulness according to Your Word, for You have sown the seed of eternity within us, the fulfillment of our hearts, and the answer to every prayer—how great are You, O Lord!

Now in the coming of dawn, after the night is nearly past, Father, we worship You, for You have borne the heaviness of our burdens and stood with us through it all. You are our comfort, our strength, and our sufficiency—and though our might is small, great are Your wonders which You have done! Surely, You are worthy, and Your gifts to us are without end. You are sovereign, allowing us to be afflicted and tested to refine us, but You have always been in control. You have never failed us—You pull us from the depths by the hand, O our God. Now, let obedience and love define us, and let us praise You forever as Your children, born again from mercy and delivered from darkness once more.

> *All the people perceived the thunder and the lightning flashes and the sound of the trumpet and the mountain smoking; and when the people saw it, they trembled and stood at a distance. Then they said to Moses, "Speak to us yourself and we will listen; but let not God speak to us, or we will die." Moses said to the people, "Do not be afraid; for God has come in order to test you, and in order that the fear of Him may remain with you, so that you may not sin." Then the Lord said to Moses, "Thus you shall say to the sons of Israel, 'You yourselves have seen that I have spoken to you from heaven. You shall not make any other gods besides Me…'"* (Exodus 20:18-20, 22-23, NASB).

True God

~ Wisdom and Grace ~

O God, surely You have founded us in Your wisdom and created the way back to You in grace; You are our greatest advocate, our strong defender and infallible Counselor, our perfect Lord! You reach into the inner depths and consume us with Your truth, ridding us of our sinfulness. Your Word defines us, and even unto death, Your mercy does not falter. Our hearts are tested to reveal their real nature and the extent of our own obedience; You are ever patient, Jesus, and You know the appetites of our souls. You are pure and holy, and Your plans cannot be moved. Your Spirit indwells us to repair our secret brokenness—You heal us, O God! You resurrect us from the dead, where once in shame and selfishness we dwelt; You are our Rock and our refuge—let us submit to You!

You restore us and will forever change us; You have made us new. The presence of Your commands, the remembrance of Your grace is ever before us. You have won us for the sake of Your victory in Your sovereign name, O Lord! You are the Almighty, Your words are tested but will always come to pass. For Your glory, Your Son pursues us with salvation, that we might be sanctified and free in You! Though we are unworthy, You have given us to stand before You in the light of Your mercy and love. You have exchanged our ruins for righteousness and our robes for unity and service, sons of the house You have built! You are intimately aware of our every need and hear all our cries; You respond in the tenderness and kindness that renew our soul.

Father, You are faithful! Do not turn away from us—no,

but You seek us when we go astray. We pray, confessing before You—please, forgive us!—and let us be as emptied vessels, ready to be completely filled before Your throne! Give us the courage to follow, our Lord, to leave everything behind. Blessed are those who have become lost and broken, who have been found by You! For even as You were abased and rejected, so too will we suffer, but our troubles are as nothing compared to what You have endured. Give us the heart to see Your glory, Jesus, even through the trials and to faithfully labor for Your sake, our Lord!

You commands are love, Father; Your truth is a shelter. You are the shield of faith that carefully surrounds us—Your hope shines brightly into the day! Surely, though You chasten us, You do so with love; You discipline us as children but deliver us, preserving us for good. Let us invest all we have in You, for a single word from You can seize us. Lord, there is nothing too great or small that escapes Your notice: You come to release the captives, opening the eyes of the blind! Draw us near to You in redemption and search our hearts; show us Your might and Your majesty, that we may be confirmed as Your children, O God! For You have given us the power of Your Spirit and of prayer to break down strongholds. Teach us, we ask, to wield it for Your kingdom—for nothing is impossible with You.

> *For it is not an enemy who reproaches me, then I could bear it; nor is it one who hates me who has exalted himself against me, then I could hide myself from him. But it is you, a man my equal, my companion and my familiar friend; we who had sweet intimacy together walked in the house of God in the throng. Let death*

come deceitfully upon them; let them go down alive to Sheol, for evil is in their dwelling, in their midst. As for me, I shall call upon God, and the Lord will save me. Evening and morning and at noon, I will complain and murmur, and He will hear my voice. He will redeem my soul in peace from the battle which is against me, for they are many who strive with me (Psalm 55:12-18, NASB).

 Clean

We come before You longing for Your presence, every day so desperately in need. We bow before You in supplication—Lord, give us clean hands and pure hearts, we pray! Show us Your glory, Father, for we have been poured out; show us Your redemptive power, that we may witness Your hand! For now all of our supports have abandoned us, but You are our rescue; we who trust in You, Jesus, will never stand alone! You are powerful and faithful, Father, an everlasting Creator who works for our good. We will be refined as silver is refined, but Your ways are higher than our ways—You are always sovereign, God! Your Word is unalterable and cannot be changed; surely, You are the same from beginning to end. Lord, You are our Savior, and Your promises never fail!

You are the One who draws us to our feet, who gives us strength when we have none; You are our protector and provider, O Lord! Even in the midst of great distress, You never forsake us. Your wisdom and love sound forth in every storm and trial, roaring out against our enemies. Let us witness it, for we will be justified and upheld in You! You will heal the broken, and Your heart cannot be persuaded from Your cause—You are the hope and redemption for us, the everlasting restoration. Surely, we will praise You yet again, O God! We come before You in gladness, for You have made us whole—there is so much You freely give us of Your compassion and strength, when we trust in You!

God, You are our confidence! In affliction, You have taught us the lessons of surrender; we are as children who submit to You, and we will obey. Father, even You have commanded us to ask, and You promise to faithfully defend us even when we are persecuted for You! You answer in Your time but with a just and perfect reply. You do not leave us wanting, and Your gracious Spirit intercedes for us, uniting us in love before Your throne. Lead us to walk in You, Jesus, that we may follow Your commands all of our days; once more, we will rest in You alone.

For You work justice for us and through Your mighty Word by the strength of Your hand and Your salvation! It is Your comfort and unshakable hope that sustains us even when we do not perceive Your love. Forgive us, Father, and let us see You ever the more in the time of need as in the coming victory, for You have humbled us according to Your goodness. Let us take hold of our new resurrection in You! In times of weariness, remind us that the war is Yours, Father, and You are He who fights on our behalf, that all strength to conquer and the presence of salvation is firmly within Your control; gird us with Your armor, that we may stand in the evil day! God, in our weakness, we surrender, and still we will trust in You. In the appointed hour, You will bring about our desire and restore us! Even in this moment, Lord Jesus, hear us. We wait for You with prayer and supplication, seated before Your throne, knowing that You satisfy.

> *Then, the same day at evening, being the first day of the week, when the doors were shut where the disciples were assembled, for fear of the Jews, Jesus came and stood in the midst, and said to them, "Peace be with you." When He had said this, He showed them His hands and His*

side. Then the disciples were glad when they saw the Lord. So Jesus said to them again, "Peace to you! As the Father has sent Me, I also send you." And when He had said this, He breathed on them, and said to them, "Receive the Holy Spirit. If you forgive the sins of any, they are forgiven them; if you retain the sins of any, they are retained" (John 20:19-23, NKJV).

Compassion

O beloved, let us remember who we are; let us take heart, for we are children of the King! Let us recall that in victory, He has overcome the dark. Yes, our God delivers us—He makes the broken whole again! He is our bulwark, and His love, protection, and sovereignty cannot be trespassed. All unkindness against the Son is forgiven, but to ignore the Spirit is the inviolable offense, for what man can succeed against His will? Our trials are temporary and passing, but our God is forever faithful and true; His revelation comes quickly, and His Word is fulfilled! His Law is perfect and unchanging; surely, He is just, and His grace knows no end. Every day is His alone, and He endows each moment with purpose—He equips us for our good. So great is His care that the Good Shepherd laid His life down for us; now, let us be restored in Him!

He is the house of our habitation; His Spirit is perfect, searching, and wise. He gives us the confidence of coming before Him because of His great love and mercy, to know the expectation of His plans for us, that we may kneel and worship before His throne! For though His ways far surpass our own, and though we cannot always see the victory at the end, indeed, He is with us, making preparations for our hearts to receive His Word! Father, we pray—hear us!—You are God, and You came to save life, not to destroy it, to accomplish Your perfect, infallible works, to triumph over the enemy! You have promised that we may come before You and ask, that we may receive; when we knock, You will open the doors of heaven for us. Father, unveil our eyes to see Your mystery, the power of what You have done!

Your salvation is forever, Father, and Your Spirit is a gift to us; we discover new mercies in You every day. Your love, Jesus, has delivered us from blindness, and let us walk in ignorance no more—let us taste of Your goodness—teach us to pray! You have given us the garments of Your praise and Your righteousness; now, disclose Your heart, Lord, for we take rest in You. Oh, we pray, draw us near to Your majesty and supernatural love, and subdue the enemy before us, Father, that we would be the witnesses of Your strength! Let the light of Your face shine upon us, for we take refuge in You, and nothing can take us, O Lord, from Your side.

> *And it happened when He was in a certain city, that behold, a man who was full of leprosy saw Jesus; and he fell on his face and begged Him, saying, "Lord, if You are willing, You can make me clean." Then He put out His hand and touched him, saying, "I am willing; be cleansed." Immediately the leprosy left him. And He charged him to tell no one, "But go and show yourself to the priest and make an offering for your cleansing, as a testimony to them, just as Moses commanded." However, the report went around concerning Him all the more; and great multitudes came together to hear, and to be healed by Him of their infirmities. So He Himself often withdrew into the wilderness and prayed* (Luke 5:12-16, NKJV).

~ The Quietude of Peace ~

Help us to perceive You, Father, and enter into Your rest with spirits wide open; help us to see with eyes that have been cleansed, for You have prepared our hearts—now gather us to You! Oh, for You have redefined us, Lord, now let us gaze upon You with glory, in thanksgiving and praise! You have brought the mountains low, and You sustain us; yes, in every moment, let us worship You! In the shadow of Your wings, You preserve us, for we are Yours. We live in You alone, in the stillness and the comfort of Your everlasting arms. Jesus, You show us the light of Your love and the depths of Your heart in Your salvation; Your knowledge and mercy are more than we can comprehend! You console us in our weariness; You fill us as broken vessels made new in You.

You are with and for us; You faithfully love us, and Your Word does not fail! Indeed, You sharpen our eyes to the mystery of the Gospel; in the hour of our utmost need, our hope is fixed on Your love! For You are active and pursue us, our living Savior, the rushing water that cleanses and restores. You are the way in the wilderness, the only love that can justify us, casting out all fear. You are peace for the unsteady and surety for the weary. Let us trust Your faithfulness—we long for the day when You will unite us as Your Spirit overflows, transforming us, our God!

Yes, and there is joy in the silence, the strength and comfort of Your hand; Your love revives us, and we treasure You as the restitution of our souls! You are the communion, Lord, the beginning and the end, our ever-present and unspoken assurance that lives inside us, our help in times of need. You are the truth and blood of salvation, which You have given freely for us. You have authority, and there is none like You! Beyond expression, we are grateful, found and captured in Your forgiveness and enfolded in Your love.

You are in our midst, O Lord, a Father's heart whose kindness and wisdom toward us is more than we can ever know. Your kingdom comes and we perceive it as You fit and equip us, grafting us in as instruments of Your chosen plan! All Your ways are holy, God, and surely You have formed a resolution for us. You have shaken the ground beneath our feet to test the rock on which we stand—now, let Your will be done! Help us to believe, to trust in You and recall Your presence, that You are always near. Even on this day, You have anointed us, and we will rejoice, for You have done the impossible—for Your glory, forever we will call out in praise, for You have remembered and saved us, our God!

Thus says the Lord to His anointed, to Cyrus, whose right hand I have held—to subdue nations before him and loose the armor of kings, to open before him the double doors, so that the gates will not be shut; "I will go before you and make the crooked places straight; I will break in pieces the gates of bronze and cut the bars of iron. I will give you the treasures of darkness and hidden riches of secret places, that you may know that I, the Lord, who call you by your name, am the God of Israel. For Jacob My servant's sake, and Israel My elect, I have even called you by your name; I have named you, though you have not known Me" (Isaiah 45:1-4, NKJV).

 Transfixed

O Lord, we stand with our hands heavenward and hearts raised to You! We are transfixed by Your faithfulness, for You stand the test of every time—oh, and how we long for Your presence to overflow! From the beginning to the end, all our days are held in You, who stood before Creation, before the universe was formed. You reached out in love and mercy to form us in Your image—God, how good You are!

In Your Holy Spirit, Your life within us, Your knowledge and wisdom pour out. Your Word speaks to us, all around us—it is a lamp unto our feet. You give us instruction and clothe us in robes of righteousness, for it is Your promise that guides us. Help us to trust in You in wholehearted surrender, O God! For indeed, we are not our own any longer, but we are Yours, Jesus, who has ascended to the throne on high. From the grave, Lord, You have paid our ransom, and You cared for us perfectly as we have waited on You. Jesus, You do the impossible with perfect majesty!

You are loving and kind, Father, rich in mercy and true, healing every harm, ministering to the wounded. You cleanse us, that we may be pure and blameless before Your throne! You speak of Your works all throughout Creation. Your children are beloved and tended in Your perfect grace. Only because of You, our Shepherd, can we do great wonders for Your kingdom—Lord, how blessed are we who trust in You! Let us enter Your rest with rejoicing and the service of Your labor with praise, boldly coming before Your throne in petition, knowing You will give us all we need. In

Your proper time, You work miracles for us—Jesus, magnify Your name!

You are so patient with us as we come to understand our own insufficiency. Let us endure, then, with tender devotion, for Your yoke is easy and Your burden light. Indeed, for though our affliction is but for a short while, even You have refined us to fit Your purposes—take us and use us as we yield to You, O God! For the sake of Your Word, restore us, for Your grace is the crown upon our heads. Shine upon us, Lord, as Your witnesses! Let us look to You—we ask that You hear us, for all of our hope is in You.

> *But Mary was standing outside the tomb weeping; and so, as she wept, she stooped down and looked into the tomb; and she saw two angels in white sitting, one at the head and one at the feet, where the body of Jesus had been lying. And they said to her, "Woman, why are you weeping?" She said to them, "Because they have taken away my Lord, and I do not know where they have laid Him." When she had said this, she turned around and saw Jesus standing there, and did not know that it was Jesus. Jesus said to her, "Woman, why are you weeping? Whom are you seeking?" Supposing Him to be the gardener, she said to Him, "Sir, if You have carried Him away, tell me where You have laid Him, and I will take Him away." Jesus said to her, "Mary!" She turned and said to Him in Hebrew, "Rabboni!" (which means, Teacher). Jesus said to her, "Stop clinging to Me, for I have not yet ascended to the Father; but go to My brethren and say to them, 'I ascend to My Father and your Father, and My God and your God.'" Mary*

Magdalene came, announcing to the disciples, "I have seen the Lord," and that He had said these things to her (John 20:11-18, NASB).

 Little/Alive

Life is for You, Lord, and everything in it—yet how are we to bear truth in grace if we do not drink of Your cup? For in You, our Savior, is the resurrection, the faith, truth, and life. Now, having known You, let us witness that You have saved us—let us testify of Your name! You sustain us, Lord, and make us new once more; so we persevere in patience, that we may follow after You!

Father, You are faithful, and there is none like You, working wonders for Your people, who loose the captives and set the prisoners free; You release us and make ways in the wilderness for us! Even in the desert, You are the fountain of life. You nourish us and teach us carefully, that we may come to see and know that You are God; we learn to live in faithfulness also, in Your love, which brings fullness of life. We put You first, Father, for to You is our vow—You are mighty to save, and all of eternity lies open before You! You read our hearts and minds in justice and are willing and eager to transform us, to show us Your compassion and the kindness of Your mercy, our God.

Let us abide in You then, Lord Jesus, heeding all of Your commands and laboring peacefully and in diligence for You! Let us hold fast to Your Word, preparing to receive You. Help us to obey confidently in Your footsteps, O Lord our God—You alone equip us; You help us in our most desperate need. We are humbled, awed, and instructed by Your majesty, Father, and the perfection of Your glory which is all around us, for who is great like You? You draw from us all impurities, teaching us with time and conviction; You unify us, Father, that we may serve in love before Your throne. Oh, and let us give thanks for Your goodness; open our ears to listen, to speak as You have commanded us, O God!

Your hear our every thought and whisper and provide for us in every concern of our hearts; You will and have saved us to act in goodness and truth for Your kingdom. Jesus, You are worthy, and You alone can satisfy! Your victory and deliverance are near, and they come quickly upon us; already, You have made the way through the wilderness. In all of this and in every circumstance, You have performed Your purposes with grace and wisdom to fulfill and accomplish Your Word.

Life, then, is for readiness, for girding ourselves with the armor of God, drawing near to the throne of His mercy. Your Word is alive and moving, Lord Jesus, breaking up the fallow ground. When we see You, then we are astonished at Your wisdom and overcome by Your power, for You and Your Spirit alone yield the fruitful harvest. God, we look to You, who has redeemed our soul! You are the strength of our hope and our portion when we grow weary. You perfect and establish us; Your children are not forgotten by You! Let us bask in Your light, we pray, and send forth Your glory—for surely life begins when we lay it down, and we surrender all we are to You.

> *Now therefore, thus you shall say to My servant David, "Thus says the Lord of hosts, 'I took you from the pasture, from following the sheep, to be ruler over My people Israel. I have been with you wherever you have gone and have cut off all your enemies from before you;*

and I will make you a great name, like the names of the great men who are on the earth. I will also appoint a place for My people Israel and will plant them, that they may live in their own place and not be disturbed again, nor will the wicked afflict them any more as formerly, even from the day that I commanded judges to be over My people Israel; and I will give you rest from all your enemies. The Lord also declares to you that the Lord will make a house for you'" (2 Samuel 7:8-11, NASB).

Wherever You Are

Wherever You are, Lord Jesus, we call to You; wherever You are, we place our lives in Your hand. For You are with us and for us, our steady shield and our defender; You cover our flaws in Your love. You protect us from lions; when we are cast down, You guard us and keep our spirits safe in Your arms. It is You alone who breaks down strongholds, casting out our fear! All of our days, let us worship our God only, for You have given Your Son in faithful sacrifice for us. O Lord, what more could we ask than what You have already done!

Wherever You are, Your voice speaks to us; it ministers in the darkness, and You are the light. You draw near those who are desperate for You, for You are our Shepherd. You lead our souls into peace and rest before You, loving the broken tenderly and healing the sick of their sin. Father, indeed, we praise You, for You make the weak mighty, though we deserve it not, and Your vows are forever. Your Word works in and all around us—Your covenant is binding, and all Your promises stand. For though we cannot see past this moment and are so quickly plunged into despair, give us to understand, Father, how much greater You are. More than our shortsightedness, give us vision to see You once more! For who can comprehend the depths of Your protection and care for us and Your perfect grace. Lord, our helplessness brings both surrender and victory—show us how to be born again in You.

So let our rejoicing sound loudly, resonantly across the wilderness; let us triumph before You in praise! For in heaven, all of our days are held in You who love us, who is even now uniting and transforming us for our good! Indeed, You have saved us through Jesus Christ, the blood of the flawless Lamb who died in our stead. Holy, holy, holy is Your name—none is worthy but You alone! Our God, deliver us; Your Word instructs us daily in all righteousness and truth. Help us, we pray, to walk worthy of the calling we have received.

We will not be ashamed who walk uprightly, fully trusting in You! When we feel alone, You never leave us; for You cannot forsake those You love. Surely, You preserve Your people, and You hear our cries. In Your time, You will complete the purposes of Heaven in us—You secure our paths and equip us, that we may continue confidently, with all hope in You! Father, we pray to see Your power, that we may witness the strength of Your hand; assuredly, it is You who are refining and remember us, our Restorer and our Healer, our Savior and our God.

> *"Hear, you who are afar off, what I have done; and you who are near, acknowledge My might." The sinners in Zion are afraid; fearfulness has seized the hypocrites: "Who among us shall dwell with the devouring fire? Who among us shall dwell with everlasting burnings? He who walks righteously and speaks uprightly, he who despises the gain of oppressions, who gestures with his hands, refusing bribes, who stops his ears from hearing of bloodshed, and shuts his eyes from seeing evil: he will dwell on the high; his place of defense will be the fortress of rocks; bread will be given him, his water will be sure. Your eyes will see the King in His beauty; they will see the land that is very far off"* (Isaiah 33:13-17, NKJV).

True God

⁓ **At the Same Place** ⁓

O Lord, You have said that Your justice comes suddenly, that in the day we cast away our idols, there will be redemption, and that Your mercies renew each morning, for You are merciful and kind. Yet Father, You have broken our foundations that were crumbling, You have torn the weak fortresses apart. Please encourage us, for You are our comfort, and let us cling steadfastly to the promise of Your Word! You are the Craftsman of Creation and our Father, always working for our good in patience and love.

For who can know Your ways unless You reveal them, and to whom will You disclose Your heart? Your purposes are Yours alone but also for the grace and glory of Your people who make Your trust their refuge. We surrender and empty ourselves, that we may be taught by You! You permit Yourself to be found even by those who do not seek You; You are the God who restores us, who changes our hearts and carries us from strength to strength. You alone have robbed the grave and trespassed in darkness, making the road to our salvation by Your obedient and sacrifice, Lord Jesus. Let us remember that You are with us, our Savior, and there is nothing too great for You!

Father, we bow before You and remember You, for Yours is the hand that preserves us and the constant love that never fails. Your heart and Your eyes ever search for us, hearkening to those in need! Let us humble our hearts, then, and conduct ourselves in patient endurance, laboring in Your truth; let us fear You only, our God, the might and force of Your majesty and Your sovereign commands. Oh, let us trust You—gird us in faith! Thank You, O Lord God, that You wage war for us; help us and keep us in Your perfect peace, who stand steadfast in You!

Soon, we shall come into Your place, for You have shown us Your wisdom; You have poured out Your Spirit to reestablish us, breathing hope into our souls! Give us a spirit that is vital, O God, for You have scattered Your people but will bring us close again. Your Word steadies us, perfects and pursues us, directing us to do all You have said. Lord Jesus, let us enter into You, taking hold of the privilege of prayer that You have allowed. The trying in the wilderness is as nothing compared with the Cross You have borne upon Your shoulders that we may be one with You in freedom. Even our trials are a crown of glory for the everlasting, Your perfect love beyond our strength that teaches us to run for You, our God!

> *My soul, wait silently for God alone, for my expectation is from Him. He only is my rock and my salvation; He is my defense; I shall not be moved. In God is my salvation and my glory; the rock of my strength, and my refuge, is in God. Trust in Him at all times, you people; pour out your heart before Him; God is a refuge for us* (Psalm 62:5-8, NKJV).

Stay

O Lord, we cannot imagine how You will act next, how faithful and mighty You are! We cannot fathom how powerfully You love us, for You are our King and our Shepherd; You have led us back to Your arms when we had gone astray! Father, You give us hope when we least expect it, grace far beyond what we deserve. You are our Keeper and our Savior, One who is mercifully loving—oh, how many have turned aside who have not known Your heart! How deep and how wide is Your love, Lord Jesus; You grieve with us in times of trial and bless us for Your glory. You are good, and there is none like You.

You tell us to wait upon You, Father, that You would renew and restore us in Your perfect time. You provide for all our needs, and every prayer has its answer—even You teach us to pray, encouraging us, that we would hold fast and learn to trust in You! You have given us strength that we may take courage in delight and joy in You. We surrender and boldly proclaim Your Word as the Law of our lives. We speak peace and blessing, yes, and victory, and it is all because of You, O God! For if we do not fall away when we are tested, then we are proven faithful to the end; as gold that is refined, O God, You are teaching us to stand in Your Word. How perfect it is to be held by Your love, sheltered close to Your heart and comforted, relying on You in our brokenness, for You can make us new again!

For every season is not meant for mourning, but Your radiant presence and testimonies of Your faithfulness define our days. O Lord Jesus, let Your kingdom come and Your will be done in every circumstance; You are the covering and shield about us, our closest companion and truest friend. Jesus, Your Word never fails, not simply because of Your name but because of Your vow that is everlasting, indeed, because of the tenderness of Your heart! How great is Your affection towards us, how abundant the fountain of living waters inside! You take us in and willingly cleanse us, for Your sacrifice makes us whole.

Jesus, now, let us elevate our hearts; even let our praises rise to You, that may we always remember the goodness of Your grace and the faithfulness of our God! Your kindness follows us, and Your mercy preserves us; Your deliverance is complete and already written—surely, You exalt the lowly, O God! In the early season, You plant us as we search for You; then You bring us to fruitfulness with a growing faith in the end. Lord, none is higher than You; as You are mighty in the heavens and working wonders, all the mountains tremble and quake before Your throne! Oh, for You have worn our iniquity upon Your shoulders: God, our need for You is the mark of Your love! In our baptism, by Spirit and by fire, by Your life, we are reborn; now, renew us, we pray, that we also may reflect You, our Lord and our God!

> *Thus says the Lord of hosts, "Do not listen to the words of the prophets who prophesy to you. They make you worthless; they speak a vision of their own heart, not from the mouth of the Lord. They continually say to those who despise Me, 'The Lord has said, "You shall have peace" '; and to everyone who walks according to the dictates of his own heart, they say, 'No evil shall come upon you.'" For who has stood in the counsel of the*

Lord, and has perceived and heard His word? Who has marked His Word and heard it? Behold, a whirlwind of the Lord has gone forth in fury—a violent whirlwind! It will fall violently on the head of the wicked. The anger of the Lord will not turn back until He has executed and performed the purposes of His heart. In the latter days you will understand it perfectly (Jeremiah 23:16-20, NKJV).

~ At the Very Last Moment ~

O Lord, at the very last, when we can do no more, You are with us; still, it is Your Spirit that comforts Your people and gives us strength to stand. Lord, we draw near to You in confidence with our whole hearts, trusting that You will restore. We look to Your holiness and Your Word which never fails; we look to the testimony with which You have equipped us for our good. God, let us offer our hearts to You and surrender freely—there is nothing else to give, for in You is all we are. You are our Father, and You love us, our God, and You will surely deliver us: You do as You have promised, our Lord!

You are the light of the morning, and we will follow You; You pour forth Your wisdom and depth into our souls. From the knowledge of Your Word, You bring life and fruitfulness; You give us gifts of discernment and the surety of Your purpose that we may know Your will. O Lord, let us rejoice, for our lives are found and continually unfolded in You! You have taken up our cause and raised Your banner over us to give us the strength and courage in the midst of all our days; You have declared Your righteousness over us and redeemed us, so we are completely set apart. Now, we pray, O Lord, take us into Your arms and receive us, that Your name and glory may be magnified!

You illumine the darkness, Father, for You have brought forth new life from the sword—Your Spirit has pierced us and shown us who we truly are. You have heard us, Lord Jesus, and what more can we ask—let us give abundant thanks that we are forgiven, our God!

The time of Your salvation has drawn near, and You have prepared us for the hour that we may listen, and You will do all that You have said. Oh, Lord, You are our eternal Savior, and nothing can snatch us from You, for Your resolution is pure. Your hope does not disappoint, O Lord, but Your mercy is our strongest comfort. Let us rejoice, for our hearts are remade in You!

In obedience, Father, let us walk in You—bring forth Your healing and hope, the strength within us to follow all of Your commands! For the sake of Your name, let us bring You glory. Let take up our Cross and finally be led by You in joy and gladness after the time of testing has gone—gird us with the armor of Your kingdom and of trust, standing on Your Word alone, that we may begin again.

For You are a Father who loves His children, and to those who seek You, You give honor and blessing. You humble us, that we may be exalted, and we will never be ashamed of our testimony in You! It is Your love alone that has saved us: You are the way, the truth, and the life.

When every piece of pride is torn from us, You replace it with meekness and submission in faith; when Your Spirit overwhelms Your people, then we are Your workers, and our lives are changed for Your glory! For though we once were strangers to You and enemies before Your throne, now, Father, You have restored our lives, and the wonders of Your truth open up as a flood. Lord, let us praise You forever, for You have established us! As You have drawn us into the deep, so You have saved us. Your love has become precious to us—in everlasting assurance, You call us home.

Now Thomas, called the Twin, one of the twelve, was not with them when Jesus came. The other disciples therefore said to him, "We have seen the Lord." So he said to them, "Unless I see in His hands the print of the nails, and put my finger into the print of the nails, and put my hand into His side, I will not believe." And after eight days His disciples were again inside, and Thomas with them. Jesus came, the doors being shut, and stood in the midst, and said, "Peace to you!" Then He said to Thomas, "Reach your finger here, and look at My hands; and reach your hand here, and put it into My side. Do not be unbelieving, but believing." And Thomas answered and said to Him, "My Lord and my God!" Jesus said to him, "Thomas, because you have seen Me, you have believed. Blessed are those who have not seen and yet have believed" (John 20:24-29, NKJV).

~ Rich Love ~

O Lord, let us be steadfast in You! Let our confidence and strength arise and be drawn from the wells of Your reserve. May we be fed in Your Word and nurtured in Your Spirit, God, that our souls would be unmoved that rest upon Your promises and the goodness of Your faithfulness—the unfailing counsel of Your love! For You are life and the way of healing, hope, and reconciliation. You cleanse us from our innermost parts to purify our soul—surely, You have not forgotten us, but we are formed for works that will declare Your glory! Even as the Spirit flows from Your lips to inform us, Jesus, You are in us, that we may know with certainty what the Father has said. You are the precious Lamb, the permanent offering that has redeemed us. You have taken our iniquities from us, and we will trust in You!

You are in the midst of the mysteries of all heaven and earth, Father, and it is Your voice, the longing for Your salvation which we hear. Your love is written into our most guarded recesses—You alone are the conquering King! You are the advocate and the Judge, the great "I AM"; Yours is the Spirit of truth that convicts of sin but also in unfailing righteousness and compassion restores us—God, let the story of our lives be that we are confirmed in grace, one in Christ with You! We surrender to Your direction, knowing that You will be with us wherever we go, for You have appointed for us salvation and will faithfully lead us; You anoint our steps. Then let us diligently seek and obey You, trustworthy stewards of Your ministry, bearing a fruitful harvest with endurance for Your kingdom, O Lord!

You are a refuge, and Your Spirit lives within us; You have carried the burden, Lord God, and Your sacrifice has made us whole. For You are able, God, and when we are broken, You uplift us. Your countenance shines upon us, illuminating our paths—forever, Lord, You transform us as the light! You esteem those who obey You and who humble themselves before You; truly, You alone are worthy and repay the rebellious and proud. Having seen the world, Lord God, having lived as man, Your commands are our shelter, and we willingly offer what You desire—the sacrifices of worship and thanksgiving, a contrite heart. For we see dimly, O Lord, but You have enlightened and washed us white as snow that we may reflect You. Jesus, we pray with might for Your knowledge—oh, how great is our everlasting God!

Let Your Spirit, then, and Your truth overtake us, for nothing is so holy as Your purposes for us and heeding Your call. We come in eager expectation, baring all we are before You throne. Strengthen us, Father, to become children again, trustworthy servants who pursue the wisdom of Your will! For You have chosen us, though we had not sought You; You have reclaimed us with a grace and mercy we have never known—You redeemed us, our God! By faith, You have made Your will known in us, so let us revere You, our Savior and our God, for Your justice and strength outlast time.

This day, which is holy to You, let us remember our Father who is good, who has saved us and received us and reconciled. Surely, You have opened wide the door that we may never be shut out from Your love! We give thanks from a heart that has been emptied, Lord, which has been surrounded and captured by Your care; what a perfect gift is Yours, God, a life which has been challenged and tested to be made complete in You! We come into Your tabernacle with our hearts surrounded, for as You have commanded, Your name endures. We come before You unworthy, but You revive us, for You alone make the broken whole again, our Lord!

> *Fools, because of their transgression, and because of their iniquities, were afflicted. Their soul abhorred all manner of food, and they drew near to the gates of death. Then they cried out to the Lord in their trouble, and He saved them out of their distresses. He sent His word and healed them, and delivered them from their destructions. Oh, that men would give thanks to the Lord for His goodness, and for His wonderful works to the children of men! Let them sacrifice the sacrifices of thanksgiving, and declare His works with rejoicing* (Psalm 107:17-22, NKJV).

 Not to Harm

Lord, You are with us; all of our lives rest in You! Your presence descends among us in the Spirit; we abide and trust in Your Word. Though we cannot understand Your ways or mark Your time, Your love and grace dwell within us forever, working for our good. Your faithfulness in the inner man confirms every pure confession of our soul, drawing us nearer to Your glorious day!

For our justification is not of ourselves, so let us respond to Your commands; we can hold nothing apart from You. It is Your blood, precious Lord, which has brought about our resurrection, through the shameless, perfect, sinless blood of Christ! No force can stop Your victory, for You permeate every corner of darkness with all-consuming light. Father, there is no relenting considering the one who has declared You in faith, for You have loved us, and Your Spirit searches our soul! You are majesty, Father, an immeasurable sovereignty across the heavens we cannot fathom. We surrender to You, trusting that You are good, and You always provide.

How can we grasp Your brilliance or ever contain You in our hearts? No, Lord Jesus, but Your presence exudes from us—Your faithfulness and justice, Your perseverance and righteous love! For though we ourselves are powerless, yet we are content in being held by You; we are at peace in Your presence, for You lead us from our captivity and set our spirits free. Never, O Lord, are we hopeless—You have not left us alone—for while we may never know all Your purposes for us, You do not abandon Your children. It is only by grace that we hold fast in You! We confess the promises of Your truth, for our God defends us. Now, in this hour, let us lean steadfastly on You.

How You must look upon us, Father, with such compassion! You sent Your Son, meek and lowly, to save us, a shelter for the weak, a blessing unto the poor. You take us in as Your children, to be one with You in the promises of Your richness and glory, set as on high—surely there is great joy in those who seek You always. Father, for Your glory, change us, renew our souls! We are but men, yet in the restoration, we become humble servants, willing before You. Oh, and comfort us, Lord Jesus as we wait on You, our great and faithful God!

You are glorious, and none is like You; we are merely sojourners here, on a journey with a purpose to seek Your kingdom and to fulfill Your work in this world. Your way at the beginning is like a whirlwind, a creation, and You stay us with mercy and justice and powerful love, a calm determination at the end. We rejoice, for our names are written in Your Book of Life; we are blessed who are pressed into Your image by the weight and kindness of Your love! You stamp Your seal upon us, and it is everlasting, given freely, O God, to those whom You have made.

I opened my mouth wide and panted, for I longed for Your commandments. Turn to me and be gracious to me, after Your manner with those who love Your name. Establish my footsteps in Your promise, and do not let any iniquity have dominion over me. Redeem me from the oppression of man, that I may keep Your precepts. Make Your face shine upon Your servant, and teach me Your statutes. My eyes run down streams of water, be-

cause they do not keep Your law (Psalm 119:131-136, NASB).

Plea of a Broken Heart

O Lord, save us, for we are not our own! We gaze upon You in wonder as little children, waiting in awe to receive all You have in store. Though none can fully understand Your times or seasons, let trust that each has its perfect purpose in Your ordained time. We are but flesh, and You remember this, that as we grow weary and burdened with trials throughout the day, You never leave our side. For You are a Father, one who is tender and slow to anger, with much forgiveness. You show us Your great compassion—now, let us see Your might, O God!

Let us rise in You, Lord Jesus, and awake in newness of life! For Your unquenchable flood of mercy washes over us, cleansing out what is impure, replacing it with Your holiness and perfect kindness, O God! You lavish upon the weak and injured Your abundant goodness; You anoint us and lead us with thanksgiving! You deliver us in all our trials and from every iniquity which has consumed us, transforming us into Your image for Your glory. Now, let us display the works of Your faithfulness, our Lord! Though we have been continually broken, let our comfort be in knowing You, and that surely, You keep every promise and will do as You have said.

Lord Jesus, even despite our deepest fears, You defeat the enemy every hour. You know all his ways and our thoughts—You know exactly how to protect us, O God. For our good, by Your grace, You are our rescue; every day, we cling to the hope and eternity that rests in You. Though our lives may challenge us, this is our blessing, that we are redeemed and sanctified with purpose in You! We surrender all of ourselves and all of our heart; we throw from us our uncertainty and fear and all our idols: God, we embrace You, for You love us to the full! There is nothing that can separate us from Your side.

Our Defender, You keep us steadfast and preserve us in Your power; let us worship You! Though every stronghold may crumble, we are held secure in Your perfect unfailing Word. As You have commanded us, so let us come, let us behold the works of Your hands—let us look up and witness Your Almighty strength, Your triumph against the dark! For those whom You have scattered, You will also return as sheep to the center of Your fold, for we are Your sons and daughters, and You have changed us; now, we live for Your glory, knowing and remembering the witness You have sent! Have Your way in us, for all our hope—everything we have—is Yours, Lord God.

You are gracious to those who wait upon You; You are the God of miracles! You command us to speak and give us wisdom; You exercise justice and righteousness in Your courts. In every circumstance of brokenness or confession, You have allowed us to be brought to this place, here before the throne of Your mercy, God, where You may save us. Jesus, we pray, as only the truth remains, show us Your mercies morning by morning by the lamp of Your Word! We rejoice greatly—no words can express Your love—for You have spoken for us; we know now that there is no life too far gone for Your grace!

All of our days, Lord Jesus, restore us and may the song of Your victory and strength rise before You as our testimony, lifting the banner of Your love, for You have worked faithful truth for Your people, our Savior and our God!

I charge you therefore before God and the Lord Jesus Christ, who will judge the living and the dead at His appearing and His kingdom: preach the word! Be ready in season and out of season. Convince, rebuke, exhort with all longsuffering and teaching. For the time will come when they will not endure sound doctrine; but according to their own desires, because they have itching ears, they will heap up for themselves teachers; and they will turn away their ears from the truth, and be turned aside to fables. But you, be watchful in all things, endure afflictions, do the work of an evangelist, fulfill your ministry (2 Timothy 4:1-5, NKJV).

 Build the Wall

Even the bird songs say, "Praise the Lord, let us rejoice," and let us give thanks to our God, who has risen us up! You have built up our walls and our foundations and crushed the strongholds of the enemy whom You have taken in hand. Now, O Lord, let us rejoice! Let us trust in You, our Savior, for You are our living God who loves us and our Redeemer—nothing can trespass Your hold!

Let us come before You in thanksgiving and offer shouts of praise; let us be glad, for You have given freedom to us—You have brought us from darkness out of captivity! You have released us, transformed us, and severed iniquity from us, O Lord; You have delivered us from this season, for You are faithful, and Your love has restored us, our King! All men will endure a time of testing when Your judgment comes; still, You enfold us in grace and mercy to the end. You are good and worthy, and Your justice is powerful, completely holy. Let us testify now of Your salvation, from this time forth and forever, boldly proclaiming Your works! For out of the surety of defeat, Lord God, You have sanctified us by the truth of Your Word. Surely, You come quickly, and like broken vessels, Your reward is with You and You fill us—oh, the miracles which You have done for us, having rent the heavens on our behalf!

You have come down in flesh and labored as a servant among us; Your Son has shown us His hands, His side which was pierced for us; there is no clearer way You have revealed the depths of Your love! Oh, Lord, we bow before You, for all Your works are perfectly positioned in compassion to change those who are Your children, to create in us what is pure—let us hope with faith, and trust in our sovereign God! For You are our guard and the gatekeeper of our hearts; behold, You are making all things new in us! You shape us for Your glory, and establish us, directing us in kindness, in paths that lead to You.

Your plan is working for us and within us; Your faithfulness never fails, for You are forming a people who are Your own! You are the God of our hearts and the fragrance of our souls that extends the aroma of Your saving grace; Jesus, Your Spirit is our power! Let us commune with You in the secret places, where Your love takes us over; let us walk in the freedom of Your transfigured life! For we come running to You, and You have caught us. You have made our legs strong and equipped our hearts to serve—so we are humbled to be called Your bond-servants, O Lord, the blessed children of the living God! You hear our requests and intercede for us, that we who live under heaven would ask anything of our Father, and it is done: You are our strength and portion; surely, every day is in Your care, O God!

> *"But now, do consider from this day onward: before one stone was placed on another in the temple of the Lord, from that time when one came to a grain heap of twenty measures, there would be only ten; and when one came to the wine vat to draw fifty measures, there would be only twenty. I smote you and every work of your hands with blasting wind, mildew and hail; yet you did not come back to Me," declares the Lord. "Do consider from this day onward...from the day when the temple of the*

Lord was founded, consider: is the seed still in the barn? Even including the vine, the fig tree, the pomegranate and the olive tree, it has not borne fruit. Yet from this day on I will bless you." Then the word of the Lord came a second time to Haggai...saying, "Speak to Zerubbabel governor of Judah, saying, 'I am going to shake the heavens and the earth. I will overthrow the thrones of kingdoms and destroy the power of the kingdoms of the nations; and I will overthrow the chariots and their riders, and the horses and their riders will go down, everyone by the sword of another. On that day,' declares the Lord of hosts, 'I will take you, Zerubbabel, son Shealtiel, My servant," declares the Lord, 'and I will make you like a signet ring, for I have chosen you,'" declares the Lord of hosts (Haggai 2:15-23, NASB).

~ **The Same Grace** ~

O Lord, to You alone, we lift our eyes! Our praises rise to You, for the victory has been won! You have set Yourself before us as a shield, the sword of the Word and our salvation. You have wielded Your power within us, for Your love will see no defeat, our God! Surely, You have gone before us, that we may trust in You.

Your love encircles us, keeping us safe as You preserve the time; for even while we cannot hold the end. which is in store, we resolve to rest in You, abiding in submission and honoring all of Your commands. Though we cannot know tomorrow, now let us return to You! You meet us in every need and do not leave us weary, nor do You let the righteous fall. You are God of the ages and the Redeemer of the night! Your likeness shines in every hour, preparing us in Your time to walk in Your glory once more.

For Your way is that of a Father; more than a teacher, You are God. You will deliver us, You who have created us in the womb, waiting for the appointed hour to provide for us just what You have promised, that our confidence may be found in hope! Oh, Jesus, let us stand upon every one of Your words for You are faithful, and You comfort us in our affliction. You reveal Yourself in Your children most clearly through trial, shining the light of Your Spirit into our hearts. You have made known to us the wilderness, that we may seek You, learning to endure until the end, where Your glory is rich and all Your mercies abound! Surely, though flesh will fail, we are never alone. Your Spirit ministers to us, and You are working Your wisdom still. You call us by name, and we will run to You—for Your words and mercy cascade over us. Surely You are gracious, Lord!

In faith and neediness, we have sought You, and this was by Your design. You have shepherded us and restored us, that we would be refined, made new and whole in You. Father, You seek to make us holy like You, in courage, that we may offer sacrifices of thanksgiving and praise. Let us bear, then, Your Word of life, Lord God, resting on the promises which You have given, that You may bring forth unity among those with a passion for Your salvation. Be exalted, O God!

We call out to You, our Lord, as we are one with You, the final perfected image of all we were created for, with our life and our future hidden carefully in You, until we may take them up again. In obedience, we bow before our God, for You are our authority. Your arms enfold us, standing beside us before the throne. O Lord, we pray, bring definition and wisdom to us, even as You prepare our place in Your kingdom, for You alone equip us for the purposes You have called us to perform. In the suffering, then we are proven faithful sons and daughters, and now, let us come to You, God, as Your disciples, knowing Your Word and Your love, which will show us the way.

> *"So when evening had come, the owner of the vineyard said to his steward, 'Call the laborers and give them their wages, beginning with the last to the first.' When those came who were hired about the eleventh hour, they each received a denarius. But when the first came, they supposed that they would receive more; and they likewise received each a denarius. And when they had re-*

ceived it, they complained against the landowner, saying, 'These last men have worked only one hour, and you made them equal to us who have borne the burden and the heat of the day.' But he answered one of them and said, 'Friend, I am doing you no wrong. Did you not agree with me for a denarius? Take what is yours and go your way. I wish to give to this last man the same as to you. Is it not lawful for me to do what I wish with my own things? Or is your eye evil because I am good?' So the last will be first, and the first last" (Matthew 20:8-16, NKJV).

~ Dayspring of Power ~

O Lord, You come as a lion, even in the last, that You may be mighty as at the first—You bring the fruitfulness of Your grace and mercy to overflow! Behold, You are doing a new thing, a beautiful and glorious work for Your kingdom—You make us whole again as sons and daughters, willing for You! Our Savior, You revive us in Your abundant love and invite us to Your banquet table; You restore our souls as we come before You, entering into Your gates with praise! No longer, O God, let us look to the past but give us only to remember the testimony and the future we have in You, the witness of Your transformation that You have done in us—for the old is gone, but the new has come!

For because of our sins, we had refused You, even as we stood against You in opposition, not knowing the fear of Your name. But now, O Lord, Your Word and Your forgiveness have overcome us; You have made us strong in Your faith! You have instructed us in Your teachings and the ways of Your faithful commands. We have seen Your goodness, and You have opened the storehouses of Your Spirit within us, releasing the power of Your purposes, O Lord! For though in our iniquity, we had fallen far, now, surely You have called us back from the grave. We confess our sins as You draw us close, and You welcome us with open arms again.

Father, Your chastening is not forever, and it is Your grace which knows no end; surely, we would have been broken entirely had it not been for the kindness of Your love! For the might of the living presence of Your Word has saved us, that we would look on You and recall Your good plans for us. How could we run so long from a God who had already found us and offered us peace to turn from our sin? Now, we know Jesus, that You are God, that Your every promise and command is true! You shoot down the proud in their abundance yet respond with graciousness to Your children in great compassion. You raise us up, that Your humility and meekness would change our strength. You know all of the enemy's ways and pursue him, that we would be ensnared no more. Yes, and the wilderness springs forth a new song in the presence of Your kindness and provision: a people who will worship You in sincerity, who will turn from You no more, but hearken to the Word of Your law, O God!

Now we see Your hope and mercy as we could not perceive them before; now we know the truth and take hold! For You, Lord, became sin for us—You have ransomed us by Your sacrifice, and by Your promise, You bring us forth! Let us walk in Your ways, for You alone are worthy; we sacrifice and lay down our brokenness with every fear. When we relinquish our needs and bring our confession, taking our thoughts captive by Your Spirit, when we trust Your Word, then only can we finally stand. For You are our refuge and unfailing fortress, our God who clears the pathways before us and pours out wisdom, joy, and the fulfillment of our hope. You have leveled the mountains, Lord Jesus, for we are Yours and saved for Your kingdom—surely, You come, and Your sword is blazing with might!

You offer freedom to Your followers, but You trap the enemy in Your hand—indeed, You are He who has ransomed us, having taken us captive back from the adversary and brought us close to Your heart! For to Your people, Your love abounds, and Your forgiveness is like a wave that crashes over us, breaking down strongholds; behold, Lord, You have made the blind man see in grace! There is nothing more powerful, more faithful or unselfish than Your perfect grace and zeal for us that we may know You! Cleanse our hearts and pour forth Your life into our souls again, O God! We return to You thankful beyond measure, for You are the fountain of life.

> *At my first defense no one stood with me, but all forsook me. May it not be charged against them. But the Lord stood with me and strengthened me, so that the message might be preached fully through me, and that all the Gentiles might hear. Also I was delivered out of the mouth of the lion. And the Lord will deliver me from every evil work and preserve me for His heavenly kingdom. To Him be the glory forever and ever. Amen!* (2 Timothy 4:16-18, NKJV).

~ The Joy of Gladness ~

In all of Your brilliance, Father, the power and passion of Your Son reveals who we were meant to be. In the painful seasons of forbearance and through the heat of trials, still, Lord, You do not neglect Your grace, nor is any circumstance beyond Your control. Your wisdom reigns sovereign, and Your love and resurrection await us—Your deliverance is near at hand! Then we will behold Your redemption, born anew in those You love, seeing Your hope for those who sought it and suffered for it long; then, oh the day comes, how we will rejoice in You! For You have transformed the old into a new creation for Your glory, meant to serve and worship You, O God!

Let us come before Your throne of grace in thanksgiving, that You would continually instruct us; for Your Word is our way, and our testimonies bear witness of Your transformation, Father, for none is too far broken for You! Let us be as children before You, we pray, simple and pure in heart; hear our cry, for You have already reconciled us— You have declared it, O Lord, Your work is done! For we had been blessed in our affliction and chosen out of love; now, how much more when we run to You in complete surrender. God, You have taught us simply to trust in You. We ask and seek You with our whole heart, that every word You have spoken would take root and bloom in us, who are as humble servants before Your throne. You have sanctified and purified us, that we may be ready and peaceful to receive You once more.

For it was selfishness and our own sin that confined us,

not Your commands, and our own injustice kept us far from You. We had become enslaved in chains we could never break, but You, O Lord, have delivered us and shattered all our bonds! Your Word has restored us, and by Your grace which has saved us, trials brought us to our knees that we would remember. You are God! Let Your perfect salvation and compassion wash over us, for all our life is in Your hands. You are the strength and vision which never fails our longing heart. Surely, Father, above all time and circumstance, You are faithful; yes, let us declare the works of our God!

> *Come and hear, all who fear God, and I will tell of what He has done for my soul. I cried to Him with my mouth, and He was extolled with my tongue. If I regard wickedness in my heart, the Lord will not hear; but certainly God has heard me; He has given heed to the voice of my prayer. Blessed be God, who has not turned away my prayer, nor His lovingkindness from me!* (Psalm 66:16-20, NASB)

~ A God Like Thunder ~

O Lord, Your resolution comes, and Your truth pours out as rain; Your voice is like the roar of clashing cymbals, the rolling thunder in the heavens which cries out! Your judgments strike as lightning—You are wondrous, O God! Then, You come in an instant, Father, fury at Your side but with mercy and love written upon Your heart. Your sacrifice yields a harvest for Your kingdom, for You forgive us and bring forth fruit for Your people by Your Spirit, which is within us—we who were afflicted shall again rejoice in You! For You had stricken us for the guilt of our ways, but You are the healing; You are the way and the light through the darkness. Oh, Lord, forgive us, we pray, for there is nothing You cannot do! You alone change the deserts into streams and the seas into dry land that we may pass through them. You only clothe us in righteousness and victory, for Your compassion knows no end.

For though we were in the wilderness of sin, taken in by the enemy and snared, God, still You saw us; You remembered us there. For You have not forgotten Your covenant to us; Your promises do not run dry! Your grace has found us, Lord Jesus, and You have called us home. There is no God like You, who pursues us; no one greater, more merciful, or more faithful in their love! Your glory is more than we can ever hold, as are the richness of the plans that You have prepared for us. Let us burst forth into praise, then, at the sound of Your name which roars about as a lion, shaking the bars which have confined us, that we may go free, ransomed from the enemy's hand! For in the morning is the breaking of Your new dawn and salvation, Jesus, and we hasten to return, for You have visited and purified our hearts; ever Your eye was upon us, and You never left our side.

Our Lord, we call out to You, with eyes and hearts poured out; Father, we pray, restore! We confess our failures in Your Spirit, we repent and willingly offer our broken lives into Your hands. We pray, take the burden from us, for it is more than we can bear, but You are our salvation and our hope, our everlasting life! We were led astray, but You have brought us near; we confess our transgressions freely, for You are the perfect, blameless Lamb! Surely, there is no doubt in You, for Your love has cast out all our fear, and You are holy! Lord, Your heart is for the needy and all those who call upon Your name, for You have rescued and redeemed us even from death! Take our hearts and mend them, and hear the voice of our supplication, for we have sinned against You, God; yet, we long for You, that we would no more run from Your love!

> *"Withhold your foot from being unshod, and your throat from thirst. But you said, 'There is no hope. No! For I have loved aliens, after them I will go.' As the thief is ashamed when he is found out, so is the house of Israel ashamed; they and their kings and their princes and their priests and their prophets, saying to a tree, 'You are my father,' and to a stone, 'You gave birth to me.' For they have turned their back to Me and not their face; but in the time of their trouble they will say, 'Arise and save us'...O generation, see the word of the Lord! Have I been a wilderness to Israel, or a land of darkness? Why*

do My people say, 'We are lords; we will come no more to You?' Can a virgin forget her ornaments, or a bride her attire? Yet My people have forgotten Me days without number" (Jeremiah 2:25-27, 31-32, NKJV).

Prepared

In our desperation, we called upon the Lord, and He heard our cry—let us receive Him soberly with all thankfulness and praise! Let us fear the Lord, for He is good, and all His ways are true. He does not leave any trespass unaccounted for but is faithful to forgive when we, who were unknowing, come to understand—then, in our every moment, let us now acknowledge our God!

In His joy, let us recall the trial; let us never forget the testimony of His grace. We had longed for Him and anticipated Him greatly, for none can stand under the weight of His hand! In the unity of faith, for the sake of His name, He has looked upon our weakness with compassion; let us pay our vows, for He has remembered us—our Savior has restored the covenant with our King! For it is not by our obedience but by His mercy, not because of our dedication but because of His love and His grace that He reconciled us to Himself while we were yet enemies of the Cross, how much more among those who believe! Truly, He has paid it all to turn us from evil, that we may walk in the light—our merciful Lord and our Holy God, let us submit to Him!

So as we have been chastened, surely we have not perished; as we have learned the wisdom of His commands, now we may follow them gladly with all our hearts. Even what deep affliction has been permitted, He alone heals that which has been allowed for our growth, a partaking in His suffering to purify us, sharing willingly as heirs with Him! As we have been refined, now we have come to know His holiness and see our God who has saved us; where pride was, now there is only humility and purpose—yes, the desire to glorify His name!

Oh, and let us greatly rejoice as victors who have witnessed the Father's triumphant love! Let us give thanks for His kindness and everlasting goodness to those who have been brought near His throne! For the Lord has ransomed us, the Redeemer of our hearts and the cleansing fire that has sanctified the Spirit within us. We have confessed our sins, we cried out of fear and shame, and He has faithfully preserved and delivered us—He has always been alongside, waiting to restore. His voice and His Word now have lent us truth and knowledge, the wisdom of discernment and His Spirit of power and love in hope. He who sits at the right hand of God is worthy, the justice and fulfillment of each of our lives, who has opened the eyes of the blind! What a gracious blessing and perfect surrender, to be loved and used by Him!

For He has not despised us, but He has declared His love for us and proclaimed it throughout the heavens; He is zealous and passionate for His children—it is good to dwell and abide in His commands. For He is the One who builds up and comforts us. Lord Jesus, for the sake of our need, pleading for Your glory, we come before You! Our Heavenly Father and Good Shepherd, seek out now those who are scattered, that we may return to You again.

> *"How can I give you up, Ephraim? How can I hand you over, O Israel?...My heart churns within Me, My sympathy is stirred. I will not execute the fierceness of My anger; I will not again destroy...For I am God and not man, the Holy One in your midst, and I will not*

come with terror. They shall walk after the Lord. He will roar like a lion. When He roars, His sons shall come trembling from the west; they shall come trembling like a bird from Egypt, like a dove from the land of Assyria. And I will let them dwell in their houses," declares the Lord (Hosea 11:8-11, NKJV).

 Find You Here

Lord, You have said that You are with us through every temptation, and in every test, You are close at hand. Now it comes, behold, let us make the way clear before You in the paths of our hearts, by Your strength, that we would be found faithful in Your sight! We work out our salvation then as those who fear and tremble, yet we cannot manage it ourselves; for Your life is precious to us, God, more than we can ever afford. Your love alone does defeat the darkness; Your power gives us the will to seek Your Word with Your might! You are working within us even now to transform us, and our every moment is held in Your gracious hands, where You draw us to Your heart in mercy. O Lord, You are enlarging the place for Your glory deep within us, eliminating any root that is unworthy, that we would be free in You again!

You are the only course that is steady in trial, the only fortress that cannot be shaken in the storm; You are the way, our Lord—our everlasting hope! When You speak, God, we silence ourselves; let us act on Your Word and live in fear and sadness no longer. If we grieve, let it be for our wrongs against You; and if we rejoice, let it be in Your gracious forgiveness and all-consuming love! You have heard the earnest voice of our supplication and our prayers before You; Jesus, deliver us no longer to the enemy for testing but into victory! In the hour we did not expect, You called upon us and found us wanting; yet now, Father, consider our hearts and teach us, show us You purposes for our lives! For we have learned from You, O Lord, to be humble and gentle in heart, for Your kindness has overwhelmed us—let us honor You!

In this season, where for too long we considered only ourselves, You are raising up a generation that will seek You. Those who are Yours will be led and faithfully follow their God, chastened and refined to speak of Your name in all knowledge and confidence, having seen the works of Your hands! Lord, we cling to Your hope; we recognize we are nothing without You! For it is no longer the day when we can speak idle words, but now is the day to put on Your armor. Teach us once more, we pray, equip us to grow in You fully, boldly, and with a proven faith, Lord Jesus, standing in Your Word! You are the living water; You protect those You love.

When violence surrounds us, yet there is safety in You; give us now, as we have been broken, to find salvation again in Your plan, to fulfill the works which You have designed. You know how our soul longs for You! We call into the darkness, God, we have taken refuge in strongholds that could never stand; yet in the childishness of our ways, we repent—forgive and restore us! Yet defend and save us, Jesus, that we may live as testimonies of the light! For soon we will see no more from afar, but we will witness; let us be as the peacemakers and the aroma of truth in this world. We pour out our hearts, thankful for Your grace, O Lord, for Your promises never fail. Search our hearts and find us as those ready and thirsting for You, hungering to be faithful servants with the supernatural love and wisdom to completely submit to Your commands! For You are a Father, and who can consider Your ways—but in love, only in love have You saved us. Above all, our God will stand!

"Look, I go forward, but He is not there, and backward, but I cannot perceive Him; when He works on the left hand, I cannot behold Him; when turns to the right hand, I cannot see Him. But He knows the way that I take; when He has tested me, I shall come forth as gold. My foot has held fast to His steps; I have kept His way and not turned aside. I have not departed from the commandments of His lips; I have treasured the words of His mouth more than my necessary food. But He is unique and who can make Him change? And whatever His soul desires, that He does. For He performs what is appointed for me, and many such things are with Him" (Job 23:8-15, NKJV).

The Bread of Waiting

Let there be an end to the weeping, a start to the rejoicing; let the weary souls be glad again! Let those who were cast into the wilderness come to partake of Your harvest, living now in peace, with rest and truth. Let there be a ceasing from distraction, a turning of the heart among those who were cold; oh, Father, let Your people who have called out to You inherit their reward, a crown of glory and completion to their prayers, fully contained in Your boundless mercies, O Lord!

Let all the people give thanks and pray in reverence—the storm is over and the battle won! For the raging winds have subsided and given way to a grace that cannot be surpassed or measured. Have You not said from the beginning that those who seek You will not be moved? Yet our hearts have shifted, and all our lives have changed to be made steadfast; yet, in every way for Your glory, You are there. You have taught us to seek the strength of our God, to see ourselves through Your eyes, as weak and helpless but beloved in You. You who lower the mountains and raise the valleys, even You are one and the same, and for those to whom You dispense Your justice early, You also send Your grace and healing, our merciful Savior and Lord!

Oh, Jesus, for Your Word is power, the saving strength of our God! It is the testimony of His greatness, the surety of Your resurrection, the witness of our God's love, the One who has given us life! For You have not made man to suffer very long, though in the affliction, we become like You, shaped in Your image; yet, You know our end and our weaknesses, that we are but dust and grow weary. Thus, then, You stand into the everlasting, that we would never fall short of You nor miss the blessing of Your mercies, the beauty of Your perfect love! God, for the way that leads to Your kingdom is narrow, and all who pass through must be tried.

Your peace and stillness descend quickly, like a gentle tide, Your Word is the balm of confidence, and Your love the grace which covers all our sin! You come not in the fire but in the quiet; You have told us that the day draws near when we will see You, that Your Word shall be confirmed. We consider it joy and mercy to know You deeper, that You who have torn us down in love would establish a better house for us, O God! Yes, let us witness Your works; we shall rejoice! For You are close at hand to those who eagerly long for You—oh, lead us, our Lord! You have answered our cries in Your perfect will and the timing of Your Word, from despair to victory. Out of deep darkness, You are our rescue—bring us into the light of Your mercies once more, where we may declare the faithfulness of Your hand! Only You, O God, who know us fully, have restored us, and we will rest in You, in the open places which You have made! Let all earth rejoice and come before You, then—and soon, we shall behold You, O our Lord and Savior, that all Creation may shout Your name.

> *"I have aroused him in righteousness and I will make all his ways smooth; he will build My city and will let My exiles go free, without any payment or reward," says the Lord of hosts. Thus says the Lord, "The products of Egypt and the merchandise of Cush and the Sabeans,*

men of stature, will come over to you and will be yours; they will walk behind you, they will come over in chains and will bow down to you; they will make supplication to you: 'Surely, God is with you, and there is none else, no other God.'…Israel has been saved by the Lord with an everlasting salvation; you will not be put to shame or humiliated, to all eternity" (Isaiah 45:13-14, 17, NASB).

Your Hand

God, only You know the hearts of men; You alone reckon us as we truly are, which is sinners desperately in need of You! For we pine for Your love and for Your Word and Spirit to be set upon our lips, the power to perform all that You have called us to—a life beyond the emptiness, our God. When You draw us close, though we had forsaken You, let us give You control; teach us to discern Your will even as newborn infants. Teach us, O Lord, when to speak and when to listen, and teach us how to love! For You hear and see us and can feel our every need, having understood every part of the circumstance. You help us whenever we ask according to Your Spirit, You guide us into what is just and right. Oh, Father, forgive us; reach out and may our broken hearts cry for You as Your Spirit intercedes for us; let Your work in us be a testament of Your glory, for Your Word alone will stand!

Far too often, we become easily disturbed or swayed—but You love us, You have longed for us; shelter us, Father, pour Your Spirit once again into our hearts, for we are thirsty for You! Under the shadow of Your wings, You preserve us; Your Spirit convicts and shows us the ways of righteousness, lighting the ground beneath our feet! Your ways are goodness and justice, mercy, love, and truth which bring praise. You will guard Your flock and set us on the heights, our God! You minister tenderly to those who are in need, You bring the proud low; You level the mighty and restore them in humility—remember us, O Lord!

Let us trust You for beyond what we can see; You are

always our Redeemer; help us to serve You faithfully, our God! We can do nothing apart from You, for You are the vine through which all our strength comes, bearing fruit that lasts in every season. Lord, lift up Your hand, and draw us to You! Remove the blinders and the shackles chained on Your people from the past; let our hope be found and shown in Your glory, Lord Jesus, for Your love moves mountains, and Your might breaks every hold. You overturn foundations, only to build again. Jesus, You are Lord, with Your banner of mercy and triumph planted over us; You steady the hearts of Your people, for in You is victory!

> *Have mercy on me, O Lord! Consider my trouble from those who hate me, You who lift me up from the gates of death, that I may tell of all Your praise in the gates of the daughter of Zion. I will rejoice in Your salvation. The nations have sunk down in the pit which they made; in the net which they hid, their own foot is caught. The Lord is known by the judgment He executes; the wicked is snared in the work of his own hands...for the needy will not always be forgotten; the expectation of the poor shall not perish forever. Arise, O Lord, do not let man prevail; let the nations be judged in Your sight. Put them in fear, O Lord, that the Gentiles may know themselves to be but men* (Psalm 9:13-16, 18-20, NKJV).

 Atonement

Oh, Lord, how You love us! We are such a world in need of You, Your children who strive in desperation, calling out in need for Your grace! Yet, You are more than enough for every man, and You alone satisfy—our reason to walk and live each day is to glorify Your name! Defend us, Father, and vindicate us against the attacks of the enemy; guard our hearts in You!

For Lord Jesus, we long for You as with the pain before a birth; keep us steadfast and strong in Your love. Let us be nurtured in Your wisdom and supported by Your Word, confident in all Your promises, our God! For You are truth, and now You have plowed the soil of our hearts; You have sown Your seed into us and cleared the paths before us, that we may walk in freedom with You—oh, establish us! When we come into Your kingdom, You have built a habitation and prepared us for it; You set us upon the Rock of Your salvation, sustaining us even to the end of days, that Your mercies would be made known.

Jesus, You have borne every sin we could ever commit, having laid it down with Your life at the Cross. You have taken the burden of iniquity from us, that we may rest upon Your shoulders, as we live to serve You, our God! In humility, we surrender ourselves to Your faithfulness, to be held in Your loving arms; like fire and like the rain, Your Word refines us—let us worship You! For You have cleansed the land at last of its deep darkness, making it undefiled for the season to come. You capture and restore us in the mercy of Your great compassion and pour out Your

Spirit freely into our hearts! We will never be left in doubt who seek You, for You bring the fruitful harvest of Your unceasing grace: all we have is Yours, O God!

Every good and perfect gift is from You, every breath and blessing, with days secure in Your hand; You alone are the way across the impassable, the hope that never fades. Jesus, Your love remains, the work completed in the impossible, the fight You have already won; for it is You who does battle, O Lord, on our behalf, that You may will in us to work according to Your way! There is no one greater than You, no one more powerful or higher, whose purposes are like Yours. We recall the testimonies of Your love and faithfulness, humbly in awe of You, knowing that so little comes by our hands! Everything that is necessary, You have already given, and it is by faith in love that we are saved!

> *"And you, son of man—will it not be in the day when I take from their stronghold, their joy and their glory, the desire of their eyes, and that on which they set their minds, their sons and their daughters: that on that day one who escapes will come to you to let you hear it with your ears? On that day your mouth will be opened to him who escaped; you shall speak and no longer be mute. Thus you will be a sign to them, and they shall know that I am the Lord"* (Ezekiel 24:25-27, NKJV).

Revolution

O God, let us give thanks, for Your glory is in Your all-surpassing grace, oh, and let Your Spirit anoint us to be washed in Your mercy, covered in Your love! Our flesh, Father, had grown weary, but now our hearts are open to Your grace, that from standing long, we now may be born again and our eyes behold Your joy! O Lord, receive and forgive us, we pray, for we had forgotten You. Surely we failed to recall our need for a Savior because of our blindness, and we were in shame. In the presence of Your power, though, Lord God, within Your sovereign hand, we fall to our knees in surrender, reminded of who You are! By utter defeat and grace without end, You have won us and readied the way.

This day, let us return to You! Let us render thanksgiving and worship before Your throne, for You have saved us—Your lovingkindness, Lord, and Your praise is everlasting! Let us, who have been humbled, look upon Your glory, for this is Your command, that we love one another and be faithful witnesses for You! To the end of our days, we will exalt You, for You have sealed for us the covenant forever that cannot be broken, Father, and You have returned us back to Your holy place. Surely Your sacrifice was for us; You have delivered us, our God!

Hallelujah, let us cry out! You have changed our songs of mourning into tears and shouts of joy! Oh, our Savior—You are the healer of all our faults, for You have reconciled the broken and redeemed the lost. Your love has ransomed and revived us—Your Word is life! For at the end comes a cleanness of heart with hands ready to serve You and a heart willing to hear and obey Your commands, thirsting for wisdom and knowledge in You. O God, let us be everlasting witnesses, living proof of Your endless love!

For You have given us character, You have woven diligence into us—You give grace to the humble and bring the proud to meekness once more. You exalt the lowly, that they may see You in order to receive their inheritance, which is blessing and purpose and the strength of Your might! Yes, for You do lead us; You are our valorous King, and we will seek You! While our hearts have been hallowed in the waiting, now we see it was only to make room for You, paving the way and preparing for Your commission. O Jesus, in all of our days, let us trust and rest in You!

We are fully Yours now, Father; there can be no other way. You have made the impassable a highway, and the heart which has been hardened, You have softened by Your mercy and changed in Your perfect grace. You are our Savior, our Lord! You have given us to gladness, even in the peace of a quieted heart—we cling to You, held steadfast and immovable in Your love! There is nothing You would not do for Your children, for we are in complete surrender to our God; for who is mighty like You, worthy to be praised! You have vindicated us; from asking to receiving, Lord, You have borne our sorrows. You are forever faithful and holy—oh, for the sake of Your name, our good, and Your glory, You have satisfied Your Word! Your light shines upon us as new every morning, and we will shrink back no more, for You are our delight. God, the living testimony within us ever leads us to give thanks to You, standing on every promise You have spoken and fulfilled. For surely, now we know that Your will shall be accomplished and that any authority or stronghold placed against You will fall; for we have trusted in You, and You have delivered us—Your ways are sovereign, our God!

> *"Many a time they have afflicted me from my youth," let Israel now say, "many a time they have afflicted me from my youth; yet they have not prevailed against me. The plowers plowed on my back; they made their furrows long." The Lord is righteous; He has cut in pieces the cords of the wicked. Let all those who hate Zion be put to shame and turned back. Let them be as the grass on the housetops, which withers before it grows up, with which the reaper does not fill his hand, nor he who binds sheaves, his arms. Neither let those who pass by them say, "The blessing of the Lord be upon you; we bless you in the name of the Lord!"* (Psalm 129:1-8, NKJV).

The Grace-Filled Life

The deeper we sink, the lower we fall, the greater is the grace of God that we will be uplifted, for the old man will fall behind! For who can be justified by the Law. There is no confidence in this, for it demands perfection, and all our hope is in Christ! By our Savior alone, we are redeemed; in His grace we are sanctified and made righteous in His pure and unchanging love! He is the God of all expectation and majesty—let us live to glorify His name! Not by any other strength but the grace of God can we follow His commands; in freedom and surrender, we receive Him. We know through His sacrifice we are transformed!

For His will is not burdensome, and His love met us at the Cross; His is the way that leads us to His eternal kingdom. In the persistent struggle against the flesh, His might and mercy stand! For where humanity fell to sin, You, Jesus, came as a faithful servant to Your Father and overcame the slavery binding us, that those who trust in our God would abide as victors, no longer held in chains! Even our hearts well up with thanksgiving in awe at Your Word, Lord Jesus, for You, our Good Shepherd, are the rest we long for. Your love compels us by the power of everlasting life and resurrection, which abides in our God!

We submit to You, our Savior, because You first loved us; You are ever-patient and kind. We are not again to return to our selfish ways, but let us commit to Your ways and trust You! Even in trials, no circumstance is without His purpose or His grace. Like the One who bore the Cross for us, so also we will be conformed through troubles, yet forever, He has overwhelmed the darkness, and victory is His, whom the grave cannot hold! Let us remember the Lord, then, and be holy, for our lives are meant to testify of His salvation; let us not glory in any treasure we have in this world but only in the true glory that is our Savior, our Father who knows our needs even before we ask and will always provide. Yes, and before we spoke a word, the Creator knew and loved us—let us be as children, running to the One who gave us life! Oh, let us revere Him for our God's mercies are great!

Who keeps a vow like God does? His covenant is for us, even His love is unshakable; we surrender with ready spirits, eager to do Your will, our God! So then, let us honor Him; let us turn away no more. Let us speak the Word of life and the testimony of all He has done for us, surely and powerfully raising the banner of His sovereign grace! For the Lord does not fail, and He moves with power for those who love Him and seek the fruit of His hand. Our loyalty and obedience, then, is to the Author of Salvation, the One who fills us, who has Himself been resurrected for us—surely, His love alone can conquer, as He is at work still!

> *Behold, the name of the Lord comes from afar, burning with His anger, and His burden is heavy; His lips are full of indignation, and His tongue like a devouring fire. His breath is like an overflowing stream, which reaches up to the neck to sift the nations with the sieve of futility; and there shall be a bridle in the jaws of the people, causing them to err. You shall have a song as in the night when a holy festival is kept, and gladness of*

heart as when one goes with a flute to go into the mountain of the Lord, to the Mighty One of Israel. The Lord will cause His glorious voice to be heard, and show the descent of His arm, with the indignation of His anger and the flame of a devouring fire, with scattering, tempest, and hailstones. For through the voice of the Lord Assyria will be beaten down, as He strikes with the rod. And in every place where the staff of punishment passes, which the Lord lays on him, it will be with tambourines and harps; and in battles of brandishing He will fight with it...the breath of the Lord, like a stream of brimstone, kindles it (Isaiah 30:27-33, NKJV).

Not What We Would Expect

We cannot hold fast to ourselves, nor to our lives or any stead surrounding us; we cannot stand in the way of God confronting sin or radically revealing His plan. Apart from Your knowledge and grace, Lord, we are nothing; only by the Cross are we redeemed and restored. You alone are the unblemished Lamb, the One who cares for us and knows the condition of our hearts. You have reached out Your heavenly hand in Your perfect will to save us, to cleanse us of every sin and make us white as snow. Our freedom is in giving ourselves completely to You, to Your divine healing and heart, trusting steadfastly in Your love, living each day in Your hand.

Jesus, You are our shield of righteousness, the faith and hope in which we abide! You alone came to shine light into the darkness, to speak direction and grace to the wilderness, to destroy the works of the enemy. You only have accomplished victory for us, which is redemption and the total restoration and deliverance of our souls. In You and through You, no force of evil can stand! Sin cannot prevail in Your presence, for it flees from You and cannot take hold where You are, nor can it steal from us the eternal, for Your love outlasts the deserts, and You turn them into streams, capturing us mightily in the trials, our Lord! We are of the world no longer, but though we are in it, still our testimony is in You, the graceful burden to share the yoke of obedience and love, being led always by Your wisdom and Your instruction, O Lord.

To follow You is to know You, and to be faithful is to do

Your Word. In every corner of our souls and every desire of our hearts, our life longs desperately for You, our Savior, knowing the expression of Your sacrifice and Your love for us! We are not meant to be empty but to be filled, not temporarily sustained by passing pleasures but to be renewed by Your Spirit and conformed to Your will. Even You, Yourself, are the living manifestation of the Word, and we are Your servants, O God! Let us walk through the door of Your mercy and forgiveness, for we are weary, and now is the time come at the end for peace, leading lives sanctified for Your glory. Be magnified in us! Let us be as lights, which shine in the darkness to witness the faithfulness of our God!

Hear our prayers, O God, at last, for You are good and delight in the voices of Your children, to draw near as we hearken close to You; You provide all we need, in Your way and Your time. Let us feed on truth and justice, then, seek discernment in grace. Jesus, You are the wellspring of life and the praise and foundation of our souls—You are sovereign and true. Our King, open our eyes to see how vast and unchanging is Your perfect love! For in the way You formed us at the beginning, to be one with You, so You continue still, making us holy. What incredible grace You give that we may freely surrender, to rest in Your kindness, O God!

> *Therefore, the Lord said: "Inasmuch as these people draw near with their mouths and honor Me with their lips, but have removed their hearts far from Me, and their fear toward Me is taught by the commandment of men, therefore, behold, I will again do a marvelous work among this people, a marvelous work and a*

wonder; for the wisdom of their wise men shall perish, and the understanding of their prudent men shall be hidden. Woe to those who seek deep to hide their counsel far from the Lord, and their works are in the dark; they say, 'Who sees us?' and, 'Who knows us?' Surely you have turned things around! Shall the potter be esteemed as the clay; for shall the thing made say of him who made it, 'He did not make me'? Or shall the thing formed say of him who formed it, 'He has no understanding?'" (Isaiah 29:13-16, NKJV).

~ Enraptured in Your Love ~

The new measuring line goes forth declaring freedom for the sanctified and redeemed, and Your people look to You in eager expectation, Lord, for You alone fulfill Your Word! Indeed, what have we to fear who trust in You—You indeed are our hope, and our lives are upheld in You! Your heart is for the broken, the needy, and the lost—You are forgiveness, the confidence of being known by You. You are near to all those who call upon Your name, even in their weaknesses, and You hear the prayers of those who eagerly seek You, that we would submit to Your love and rejoice in You, our God!

For Your paths are written and established for us; they lead us in everlasting truth with justice and mercy. Though we waver, Lord, You never fail, and You fulfill every promise that You have spoken—You revive us, our God! For Your Word is like the morning dew that washes over us; oh, we pray, cover us in Your love which casts out all fear and in Your grace, which releases us from the snares of doubt. Let our hope also arise in You. As You long to provide for us as our Father, let us become all the more aware of Your presence, that we may we never lose sight of Your purposes and Your hand, which is not too short to save!

Your mercy is more than enough—You have conquered the grave for us, our Savior! Teach our hearts to receive Your Spirit, and let us walk faithfully in You. Give us the strength to seek You first and Your righteousness, to trust You completely in Your promise and at Your Word, which never fails! For You are patient and long-suffering in kindness: pour out Your love, we pray, and remember Your covenant towards us! For we are weary, but You lead us with victory and praise upon our shoulders, recreating us as new vessels fit for use and radiant with Your glory, O God. Capture us once more in Your perfect love, for You alone heal and restore us—hear us and deliver us, our Father, for You come quickly for Your servants, who are tenderly beloved by You!

> *Is it not yet a very little while till Lebanon shall be turned into a fruitful field, and the fruitful field be esteemed as a forest? In that day the deaf shall hear the words of the book, and the eyes of the blind shall see out of obscurity and out of darkness. The humble also shall increase their joy in the Lord, and the poor among men shall rejoice in the Holy One of Israel. For the terrible one is brought to nothing, the scornful one is consumed, and all who watch for iniquity are cut off...* (Isaiah 29:17-20, NKJV).

 Priorities

O beloved Lord, let us not look elsewhere for satisfaction, but let us be drawn to You! Let us consider Your greatness and yield the sacrifices of thanksgiving in return. Help us, O Father, to remember that distractions come not by Your hand; give us wisdom, Lord Jesus, that the enemy's attacks to separate us from You would end up empty, and we would rejoice for the sake of Your name instead! Let us cease striving, then, and listen, remembering in every storm and chaos and confusion that You are there. You are sovereign, with Your hand above all the works of heaven which minister down to those on earth! You are worthy, Lord Jesus, deserving all our praise and every devotion, seated at the right hand of God and victorious upon His throne!

O Lord, let us recall that every good and perfect gift is from You and that challenges and afflictions shape us for Your glory; surely, these bring a witness to You that grows much fruit, for You are the strength to the weak. For though the way is long and the road seems unsure, You are steadfast. Let us not be dissuaded but trust in Your mercy, knowing that You have carefully allowed it for our good to draw us to You, that we may know and seek You once more, O God!

Your testing will not endure forever, but You are the recollection of our hope! In the end, You will help us to stand, that we may be saved in You. Even in the most trying of obstacles, You are making us whole in Your image, reforming us for a future built mightily on Your Word and glorious with the beauty of Your light! Let us not forget,

Lord God, Your precious sacrifice, that You have overcome the grave and done so in mercy, on our behalf!

For who in heaven is like You; You never leave us alone. In everything, You bring the growth, and You do not let the search be endless, nor do You tarry long. You are always near, and You give us courage. In our progress, let us yet confess our weakness, for the night comes only to unfold Your season, to bring the harvest, O God! Only by Your endless power and Your tender and perfect love, have You adopted us—we are not without You in any trial! We are Your Creation, and You understand us; You establish us, O Father, as children of Your Word.

So often we look to You in fear, O God, but let it now be with a tender reverence of thanksgiving and praise. You know us and love us and try us—You see our hearts intimately, and we will place faith in You! For there will come a time when our faith will be tested, Lord, but that is what makes it true. Purge us of our sins and our iniquity, remove them far from us, God, for we long to be faithful servants—let us reflect a testimony that brings glory to Your name! For You complete what You have begun and have renewed us and restored us in Your strength. Let the morning come when You have gifted us for Your kingdom to accomplish Your will, that we may walk in Your ways, O God.

> *The grass withers, the flower fades, because the breath of the Lord blows upon it; surely the people are grass. The grass withers, the flower fades, but the word of our God stands forever. O Zion, you who bring good tidings, get up into the high mountain; O Jerusalem, you who bring good tidings, lift up your voice with strength, lift it up,*

be not afraid; say to the cities of Judah, "Behold your God!" Behold, the Lord God shall come with a strong hand, with His arm shall rule for Him; behold, His reward is with Him, and His work before Him. He will feed His flock like a shepherd; He will gather the lambs with His arm, and carry them in His bosom, and gently lead those who are with young (Isaiah 40:7-11, NKJV).

About the Author

Lindsay Fait is an evangelical Christian committed to spreading the Word of God. She has a passion for teaching, writing, nature, and travel, and a heart for reaching adults and students of all ages with Christ's love. A University of Florida graduate and tutor specializing in English and history, Lindsay is continually motivated by the dependent, reconciling, and forgiving relationship between God and His people.

To learn more about Lindsay's mission and receive weekly encouragement to your inbox, connect online at knowthefather.weebly.com.

www.ingramcontent.com/pod-product-compliance
Lightning Source LLC
Chambersburg PA
CBHW030337100526
44592CB00010B/717